James X

Gerard Mannix Flynn has worked in
the arts for almost thirty years. As well
as writing the novel *Nothing to Say*, he
has also worked extensively in the per-
forming arts both on stage and in film.
He is a member of Aosdána.

For Susan

GERARD MANNIX FLYNN

James X

THE LILLIPUT PRESS
DUBLIN

First published 2003 by
THE LILLIPUT PRESS LTD
62–63 Sitric Road, Arbour Hill,
Dublin 7, Ireland
www.lilliputpress.ie

A CIP record for this title is available
from The British Library.

1 3 5 7 9 10 8 6 4 2

ISBN 1 84351 029 4

The Lilliput Press receives financial assistance from
An Chomhairle Ealaíon / The Arts Council of Ireland.

Set in 11.5 on 15.5 Granjon with GillSans display titling
Printed in Ireland by ßetaprint of Dublin

FOREWORD

In 1983 my novel *Nothing to Say* was published. The story dealt with a child who had been sent away by the courts to an industrial school in the West of Ireland. Even at that time, these industrial schools and reform schools were places that sent a shudder of fear through Irish society. They were situated in the heart of Irish towns and villages and many people must have known what went on there, yet nobody openly talked about it. Nobody talked about it at all. *Nothing to Say* put into the public domain a story of child abuse at the hands of State employees and religious orders. For me, it was a fearful time. Nobody really talked about sex, never mind child sex abuse, and to level the accusation of abuse at the State and the Church and their religious congregations was an outrage. There were some people who defended the book, but many more disregarded it, and me. Since *Nothing to Say* was first published, many people have talked to me about their childhood and the abuse that they suffered at the hands of those who were entrusted to care for them.

Twenty years on, Irish society is on the verge of moral bankruptcy. The Catholic Church and its congregation is breaking up upon its own rock, by its own hand and deeds, by its own lack of honesty. It is nothing more than floating débris and all that keeps it from sinking down into the darkness is the tissue of lies and the frightened faithful who cling to these lies. The issues brought up by *Nothing to Say* are still unfinished business, unhealed wounds.

James X is the story of James O'Neill from *Nothing to Say* over thirty years on. He stands in the High Court of Ireland waiting to be called to the witness-stand to give testimony about the events of his life at the hands of the agents of Church and State: a Church that profited from the forced manual labour of 150,000 children, and a State that supplied them with these child workers. As James waits in the court building he is handed a file that has been compiled on him over the previous forty-five years. He is devastated to read that since he was three years of age he has been condemned by doctors, psychiatrists, psychologists, probation and welfare officers, who wrote report after report damning him to a life of horrendous abuse.

For the most part, these reports are rife with indifference, inaccuracy and casual prejudice, and since James knows the State doesn't consider him important enough to be a special case, he realizes that files like this were written about tens of thousands of Irish children, working-class children, and that it was on the basis of these reports that many of them were sent away. This is not James's story, it is the story of all the children that went through to rooms of hell and horror in institutions run by the congregations of religious Brothers and Nuns, under licence of the State. It is the story of those who suffered in these cruel places and those who were witness to that suffering. We all had a childhood. Let this be our common bond when we read *James X* or *Nothing to Say*.

As the character on stage is reading the reports, he realizes that he can expect neither justice nor vindication from a State that so wilfully abandoned him. The prejudicial State file doesn't tell the story of his life as he remembers it, and while he waits to go into court, James begins a quest to rescue his own story. While standing firmly in the present, he re-enacts the past and, in the process, he learns to care about and love himself. This, he says, is his reclaiming mission. Its objective is 'to thine own self be true'. The truth will set you free.

GERARD MANNIX FLYNN

August 2003

ACKNOWLEDGMENTS

The Abbey Theatre, Aosdána, Susan Bergin, Brian Bermingham, Pam Brighton, Fergus Byrne at Temple Bar Properties, Pat Byrne, Liam Carson, the City Arts Centre, Shane Connaughton, Eugene Connolly, Jack Cosgrove and colleagues, Catriona Crowe, Dubblejoint, Paddy Dunning, John Dwyer and Geraldine, Declan and Breda Falvey, Michael Finucane, Sandy FitzGerald, Sheridan Flynn, Fubar, Bernard Griffin, Gill Hall, Garry Hynes, Juice, Kearney and Melia, Garrett Keogh, Phillipa Kidd, Stephen Kingston, Sean Lawlor, The Lilliput Press, Bernard and Mary Loughlin, Gerry Lundberg, Martin McCann, Ted McCarthy, Fiach McCoghanill, Niall MacCormack, Ann McCrory, Declan McGonagle, Riona McMonagle, Annalisa McNamara, Aislinn McNamara-Flynn, Brian Maguire, Jeremey Massey, Chris Meehan, Paula Meehan, Kevin Melia, Conal Morrison, Biddy Mulcahy, Ulick O'Connor, Faith O'Grady, Agnes O'Sullivan, Fintan O'Toole, Perry Ogden, Project Arts Centre, Julian Pugh, Mary Raferty, Sarah Share, Christine Sheridan, Marsha Swan, South Kerry Partnership, Talbot Grove, Temple Bar Music Centre, Nicky Topping and The Sugar Club, Tyrone Guthrie Center, Willie White, Ronan Wilmot, Aoife Woodlock, and my parents and family.

James X

SETTING

A waiting room in the Dublin High Court, 2002.

CHARACTER

James, a man in his forties, enters the room.
He carries a file containing State documents relating to
himself and at various times throughout the play
he reads reports from this file.

PART ONE

Nearly time to take the stand, raise my hand, place my hand on the book – the best seller of all time – and swear to tell the truth, the whole truth and nothing but the truth, so help me God. Do you hear me God, I need help. The honest truth will set me free, that's what me therapist said yesterday. She got 65 euro for that. I have to go into that courtroom soon, into my past. Tell them what happened back then when I was eleven, but I just want to run and run and run. Abandon the whole thing. Fright, me therapist called it. We get it the first day we are born. Fright. I got a great fright when they handed me my file this morning but it was nothing to the fright I got when I read it. I feel contaminated, sick, soul-sick. According to this State file I was a dangerous person at three years old.

Developmental history: The birth was normal; the boy was nine pounds and bottle-fed. He sat at four months, walked at a year, was talking at a year and a half and toilet-trained at two. He started school at three but was a problem to the teacher from the start as he was always fighting with other children.

Walking and talking at two, running amok at three. Now the same people who wrote that are waiting for me in that courtroom. The order of St John of Gods, the child guiders,

13

the judge, the jury, the Probation and Welfare, the Department of Justice, Equity and Law Reform, waiting for me to perform. They'll be eyeing me up to put me down, those educators from the Department of Education, the Christian Brothers, the Oblate Fathers, The Sisters of Mercy, the Church, the State, its servants and agents, its barristers and solicitors. I'll be facing them and they'll be facing me – nothing between us but truth and denial, honesty and dishonesty. They are all around me. Everywhere. I am surrounded by them. They're in my file, in my head, in my past and now they are waiting in my present. Fright, fight, flight.

Oh God I am frightened today in this place and this moment. They have taken everything away, even my name. Today, for confidentiality reasons, I am to be known only as James X. I'm taking a case against them. Looking back, recalling to recover.

The plaintiff's claim is for damages for personal injuries, mental distress, nervous shock, wilful assault and batter, etc. etc. James X versus the State, its servants and agents, the Church and its servants and agents.

Lord help me think. Help me feel, help me remember what I don't want to remember. Help me relive what I don't want to relive. Save me from denial.

There's me legal team over there, Plead Guilty and Sons. What's that you say – there's a backlog? Justice is delayed, I can't go into the courtroom just yet. So I'll tell it my way, to myself. I won't delay. I won't abandon myself. I'll reclaim myself, myself.

I will begin at the beginning. When my father made his exit from my mother's vagina after ejaculation, I, me, was on my way. For nine months I eclipsed in my watery cave, evolving non-stop, growing cell by cell, forming in unity within the walls of my universe. I lay suspended, secure. Every moment was new, for the first time, the very first time. The faint sound of something in the far-off distance, yet ever so near. Bum-bum, bum-bum. Signals, coded messages, my first friend. The heart. Strong, pumping, never-fading, calling me out to play.

It was time, that time had come. I turned ever so gracefully in my mother's womb. Head first, nose down, I began my descent, my disconnecting began. Nature's labour locked us both in unity and combat with life's turbulent forces. 'No smoking please.' 'Fasten your safety belts.' 'Your life vests are under your seats.' 'We are coming in to land. Arrival time any moment now.' Scream! Time wants me like a vampire's lust for blood, its force is stronger than the full moon's hold upon the ocean's water. Disturbed from my slumbers, awakened by slight tremors, I kick out I contract. I kick out, I contract. I kick out I contract. The sound of the beating heart is lost to me. I am alone in a storm and I try to cling to waves. The volcanoes have erupted, a major earthquake is in progress. Strife, civil war, guerrilla war, car bomb, world war, cold war. Labour pains in sweeping waves, not unlike the first nuclear strike. Meltdown. Blackout. Curfew. Full alert. I switch to autopilot.

In my watery cave I prepare to eject. There's no going back, labour pains, it's a constant attack. The river, the river, the river has burst its banks. Hydraulic doors open wide, dead ahead, twelve o'clock, the welcoming mouth of the river. I fear it's a waterfall. The rapids await me. It's sink or swim. I don't want to leave. I don't want to go. I kick, I wriggle like a fish out of water. I am being pushed, pushed. Force upon force. Harder, harder, to the limits. The agents of time are all around me, weakening my resistance. For an instant I hear that strong pumping heart, fast, then faster still. What does it say? Its echo repeats, bouncing, ricocheting faster than light around the walls of the womb. Mother Nature has her way. I broke the code just as the last broken waters leave the mouth of the river. It reads, 'Mayday! Mayday!'

Exhausted, I cry out the last silent sound, high frequency, beyond the sound of the whale. 'Let me be, let me be.' I was being squeezed like the last bit of toothpaste from the tube. I was bollixed. I could no longer hold the fort. Like a spy submarine caught in a net, I had to surface. My final painful movement towards my first appearance had begun. Ejected, now I am on my way. Crossing frontiers of blood, pain, blood, sweat, water, sweat. Labour, override labour, labour, labour, harder, harder. No override labour, scream, scream, screaming. All systems go, switch to Earth time, five seconds, four seconds, three, two, one, touchdown.

Mayday. Mayday. Mayhem. I am across the Great Divide. I am immediately hung upside down. There is no sound, no signals, no messages from my friend the heart. I refuse to acknowledge, not one sniff of air would I breathe in. I hung undignified, mourning the loss of my companion. A slap, a sharp sting shot through me. Time had begun for me, I was moments old. The sharp sting of a slap shot through me again, like the last cutting blow from the axe upon the sturdy tree, and as it falls to the ground, it cries out through its leaves, limbs and branches its last farewell. On the day that I was born I let loose with all my might an angry hello.

P.S. Fuck you Dr Spock.

What an appearance. I trust my fellow babies in the hospital weren't too traumatized. Oh! By the way, my name is James, I am a few weeks old and have just been baptized. I've been saved from hell! Original sin's got the boot. The slate's clean. If I die now, it's first class, non-stop, straight to Heaven.

'Clap hands till Daddy comes home. Clap hands till Daddy

comes home.' 'If you're happy in your nappy, clap your hands. If you're happy in your nappy, clap your hands.' 'Who's a good boy then, who's a good boy then.' 'Goo, goo, goo goo.' 'No, no, no, that's very bold – you're not to play with that, naughty, naughty, naughty.' 'Push the button, pull the brake, down comes a chocolate cake.' 'Dirty, dirty, pooh, pooh, pooh, who's a dirty boy then? Who's a smelly boy then?' 'Do you want your bottle?'

I could say nothing, do nothing. I lay helpless looking out from my pram day after day. Frightened, frightened, lost, I just watched these strange faces, unreal shadows, my family. I hadn't a clue what was going on. Sipping milk from a titted Guinness bottle, eating Farley's rusks, munching Liga, passing yellow excrement, litres of urine. No Johnson's Baby; no liquidized Heinz baby food, no nursery rhymes, no Fisher Price, I do not like Ambrosia Creamed Rice. Helpless, there was no choice. No cabbage patch stinging like burnt flesh from a nappy rash. Call Ma-ma. Call Da-da. Call Ma-ma. Call Da-da. I'm a wind-up toy in a wound-up world. I bash my rattler off the side of my pram, Wham! Wham! Mam, Mam. A hand stuffs my mouth with bread and jam. I know it's silly but I play with my willy. Hooray. Hooray I can use my potty but I cannot wipe my arse.

Sitting in shit, surrounded, watched, minded, guarded by my sisters. Strapped in a harness. Handcuffed in a pram. Out for walkies through the street, through the park. 'Lovely baby.' 'Beautiful child.' 'The image of his father.' 'The spit of his mother.' The circus all around me – cars, buses, millions of faces, making faces, pulling faces, acting like children for my entertainment, frightening me, making me cry.

Staring at birds with the fascination of a young kitten; ears cocked to action like a cautious reindeer at a drink pool, I drink in the sounds of my world. The soundtrack is intense, constant, on and on, never-ending. I am sprouting, growing in the city among the skyscrapers. Ground level I begin to crawl. Discovering the dirt floor on all fours. I want to know everything, go everywhere, feel, touch, smell, taste. Down here, me and the cockroaches see eye to eye. Discovering, discovering, uncovering my world of wires, pliers, cups, hiccoughs, fuck ups! Shoes, socks, tick-tock clocks. Public bars, chocolate bars, buses, cars, drinking tea from cracked jamjars. Watching Mammy fight with Daddy, Daddy fight with Mammy. I am frightened of the boogie man. Creeping, crawling all around the flat. Playing with the water in the toilet bowl. Bumping my head, cutting my knee, Mickey Mouse does nothing for me. Cinderella has her fella, while my nappy is smelly and the colour's gone yella. Worn-out lino for a yellow-brick road. Disneyland and Donald Duck are a con. Happy, Happy, Happy Birthday, I've just turned one.

Hold on just a moment. I have an idea that will save me time. Being a baby is boring and painfully frustrating, also I have a pain in me bollix from nappy rash. Time to call a halt. Stand on my own two feet, so to speak. So here goes. I'm one, I'm two, I'm three, I'm four. I'm walkin', I'm talkin', I'm up off the floor. Walk, talk, walk, talk, walk, talk. No longer strapped in my Pedigree pram, my hands all sticky from blackberry jam. No more nasty nappy rash nor teething pains. Gimme, gimme air, I have broken my reins. Oh don't you stop me, no don't you dare. As I rose, stretched out, expanded in all directions, my place, my space, even my titted Guinness bottle was taken. You see Ma would leave sometimes. I would cry, not knowing where she was. Then she would appear suddenly like a miracle with a new baby. 'Where did you get it?' I'd ask, happy to see Ma back. Without any expression on her face she would reply,. 'Under a head of cabbage.' I could sense Ma wasn't happy, but I couldn't understand why. Maybe it had something to do with Daddy being down in the pub. Funny, you know, I can't ever remember, not once, seeing them kiss, kissing, holding hands, just fights, shouts, police and partings. My father going out of the house to live in the hostel for men. I hated my dad being there. 'Daddy, daddy, daddy!' I couldn't say it, 'Don't go!' Ma would be screaming at him. I hated looking at my dad's face, hurt, hurt, hurted. And my mother's twisted horribly with pain, frustration and anger.

My older sisters would cry, 'Stop Mammy, stop Ma, please.' I wanted to run. Everything would get so frightening, just like the dark. The neighbour from next door would come in. One of my older sisters would run down the stairs to me uncle's flat, telling him to come up quick, that Ma and Da were eating each other. Poison. That's it. Everything was like poison, when the venom poured out, filling the rooms of our flat, spilling out onto the landing, giving every passing body, every laced nylon curtain, an eyeful and an earful. When I was four, barely up off the floor, I wobbled and cried for a long time when Mother and Father roared.

My mother said to my father: 'You dirty poxy pig you. Get out of my house. You filthy stinking swine, you're nothing but a louse.'

My father replied: 'Oh go on you animal's cunt, you, with your dirty pox-ridden mouth you wouldn't be served in the jungle. You've a dangerous mouth when you're full of stout. You Lagan brass nail you, you'd crucify Christ if you got the chance; I'm getting out of this kip-house, where's me clock and working pants?'

'Mammy! Daddy! Mammy!' cried my older sisters. 'You're making a show of the house.' The children are frightened stiff like the elephant of the mouse. 'Daddy go, Mammy stay. Quick Daddy listen, the sirens, the police are on their way.' The baby screamed louder than the police sirens.

The new baby's ears were close to Mammy's heart, it must have woken suddenly on hearing it break apart. Wrapped in soft yellow cotton, the screams of Madeline who suddenly wakes locked alive in her nailed coffin. The horror of the House of Usher is real and I wish this was the Mansion House, I wish it was the House of the Rising Sun, I really, really wish it wasn't my house. 'So hush, hush little baby, baby bird, rock, rock, rockaby. Mammy and Daddy's little pride and joy.' Lost sheep of Little Bo Peep, go now, go, go to sleep, to peace, while all around you tears itself apart. Baby darling it's going to be OK, the police are here to take Daddy away. Now it's us little sheep that have lost Bo Peep.

Then they put me into a car zoom zoom, beep beep over O'Connell Bridge, past the Ha'penny Bridge, along Capel Street Bridge. All alone all along the Liffey I cried like the canal to the gates of Goldenbridge. At Goldenbridge, the nuns said that they were my sisters now. 'Now, now, stop that crying or we'll give you something to cry about. Christ didn't cry. Christ wasn't a whinger.' I cried, I screamed for me ma, yelled for me da. Then all the kids there started to cry like me. We screamed through the clatters in the face, the lashes across the back of our legs, the smashing of our heads against the doors.

'Mary is our mother now and God is our Father. Repeat, Mary is our mother now and God is our Father. 'Tis the Divil that has you all crying. 'Tis the Divil so that we'll be getting out of here, only the Divil. James, that's a lovely boy's name. Stop that crying now. Silence is golden, boy and girls. Silence is golden. St James, a lovely saint.'

I rocked back, I rocked forward. I rocked in silence for a

day, for a week maybe two. I cried until I was dry. I bit my lip; I bit my nails; I pissed the bed; I rubbed my eyes; I bit the boy beside me, I bit the girl beside me. They both bit me back. The nuns and the priest battered us all. Screamed at us that we were bold and evil and that they were going to put us into the washing machine to wash our souls of sin, souls of sin, souls of sin. Now it is us little sheep that have lost Bo Peep, looking for Bo Peep. I rocked back and forth till one day somebody came and picked me up into their arms and took me back to my home, to my ma, to my da and all the family and another new baby.

To whom it may concern: this statement confirms that the following information is the only information recorded in the Mercy Congregational Archives: James X of 2 Connolly House, Dublin was in St Vincent's Industrial School, Goldenbridge in Inchicore, Dublin, 1964.

Silence is golden, golden, in Goldenbridge. Sssh.

In national school – I cried, shat in my trousers and pissed myself. Not once but many times. That's how I learned to count. 'One and one is two,' the teacher would say, 'Who did a pooh? Two and two is four, which boy peed upon the floor?' Inevitably the whole class would look where the teacher pointed her finger at me. The worst part was not the pissin' and the shittin', but when the whole class led by Miss would rub it in, so to speak. It was around that time that I made direct contact with the Holy God: 'In the name of the Father, and of the Son and of the Holy Ghost, please stop me shitting in me pants the most, God. Amen.'

In a day back then it was like this: 'Pip, pip, pip, pip, peeeep. Good morning, you are listening to Radio Éireann. Over now to the newsroom for the seven o'clock early morning news.' The food-press door slammed in the living room. Ma's angry voice drowned out the news of an air strike deep in

Vietnam. 'There's no fucking milk again.' I lay in bed, the top bunk. Still, half-breathing, dead, invisible. Like reconnaissance in the dugout in the bowels of an uncharted jungle, I listen like radar.

I lay just under the bed covers, camouflaged, pretending deep sleep. Playing dead. Beside me, pressed against the wall, my two younger brothers, stuck together with sweat like Siamese twins. I lay on the edge held together by my sweat which stuck me to my brother's back. Down the other end of the bunk lay two or was it three related bodies. Under the blankets my legs were cramped, intertwined among four other pairs. Spaghetti junction. In the bed beneath it was the same. Ma's bed – 'a double Odearest, I'll have you know' – was against the wall nearest my feet. It sank in the middle. Its spine smashed from the cargo of many sleeping bodies – how many I do not know. The bed and its contents looked like a makeshift life-raft, overloaded hopelessly.

There was no air in the room. The atmosphere was that of a dense jungle, humid, suffocating, deadening, dripping, sweating, close, very close and sticky. The slight smell of sour body sweat, like that of newborn babies who lie wrapped in layers of blankets, protected from the fresh morning dew. The smashed spine of the decaying bed creaks, the contents turn in their sleep. It triggers a reaction like eggs hatching, they are breaking from their shell, they are breaking from their shell of deep sleep. 'Black tea, black tea, fifteen poxy bottles of milk a day, and all I get is black tea.' Ma's angry, fed-up voice startled me. I took extra care, I did not fancy being dragged out of my warm bed. I could hear Ma slamming the food-press door, feel her lioness temper rise. Anyone or anything that walks into the living room now will definitely be eaten alive. Not wanting to be her first victim, I slid down under the covers of my bed, like an otter slips beneath the water's surface for safety and protection.

Deep in my dugout my unease and feelings of fear disappear in my encaved darkness. There I lay in wait until the coast was clear. Half-dreaming, half-asleep, hanging on in there for the life of me. My little space, one pillow shared by three heads in a bed for two, but has six. I am part of a puzzle. A human jigsaw. I lie awake, I lie asleep, the orchestra overture begins to stir, the opera coming in like thunder, smashes, clashes. Good morning to the world, just like this, we jump like kamikaze pilots out of our sleep, me, me brothers, me sisters, ten, twelve, fifteen live wires crossing each other, energy, electric like this. 'Wake up! Wake up! Get out of bed.' An air raid in an air raid shelter, all hell breaks loose.

I try to move quick before the others hit the floor, before the scramble. Shirts, socks, jumpers, skirts, shoes, knickers, Y-fronts lie bodiless and lifeless on the floor. Quickly, frantically, my hands rummage through the clothes. I try to cover my birdy. Faster, faster. As quick as quick they're coming out of their sleep, they're coming out of their trenches. I grab a pair of Y-fronts. By the time I put them on it's a war front. The Charge of the Light Brigade. The Storming of the Bastille. The pushing, the shoving, like little turtles running for the water, for cover, they grabbed their clothes.

'Aggh, who robbed me shoelaces?' 'That's my shirt.' 'She's got my underpants on.' 'They're mine.' 'That's his.' 'They're hers.' 'You're standing on my toe.' Push, shove, kick, punch. Kill to dress, not dressed to kill, kill to dress, not dressed to kill, all 'cause the pope wouldn't give out the pill. I hate this house! Half-dressed, three-quarters-way dressed, fully dressed. 'Aggh! This water's freezin', this water's cold.' Big sister kicks me. 'You're far too bold.' 'Mammy!' I yell. 'Daddy!' I scream. Tell me friend, is this a dream? 'Hold still,' I am told, 'hold still, you pig,' while they comb my hair out, out, out from my scalp. 'Aggh!' I hate my hair being combed. Hate, hate, hate washing my neck.

Food is on the table. We devour it well and able. 'I want toast.' 'I don't want tea.' Cornflakes crushed under feet. The noise of an army marching upon gravel. I sit. I listen. Wired, wired, wired. Wired to the moon all of us. Somebody spits cornflakes across at somebody else. Someone says, 'Give me back my shoelaces.' 'No I won't let go of your hair.' 'That hurted,' I cry. 'I'm not going to school, I'm running away.' 'Get the fucking milk yourself, you old cow.' Everybody on top of somebody else. Commands, orders, hemmed-in, pinned down, no let up just let down. Sit up, stand up, turn round, shut up, speak up, wash face, hands, neck, feet, clatter. 'Wait till Mammy comes home you little bastard, you deliberately broke the comb. You're going to be sent to the bold boys' home. Right everybody, get ready for school, and don't, don't you start acting the fool.' 'Do you hear me, are you listening?' 'What did you say?' 'Take that you.' 'This is for that, you.' 'That is for this, and here, come here, I owe that to you.' 'Now shut up crying, there's the bell for school, it's ten to nine you swines.'

We are fretting, crying, upset. Half-awake, half-asleep. Scattered sheep of Little Bo Peep. Bo Peep. My little brother's got his shoes on the wrong feet. I've got my shirt on inside out. Me sister forgot to put her knickers on. Her communion dress is in the pawn. The bell for school is long since gone. I hate this house! I hate this house! I wish, I wish, I wish that it was the House of the Rising Sun. But the bell for school is long since gone, the screams and shouts of 'Come on, come on.' With holy water we bless ourselves, then we close the hall door behind. We head to school a shambles. The blind leading the blind. In the name of the Father, Son and Holy Ghost, me sister clatters me the most, and me teeth are black, black, black from charcoal toast. By the scruff of the neck and held tight by the hand we were forced, marched to school. Fuck the Father, Son and Holy Ghost, I can't take this being clattered the most. So just like that I break clean and free away, leaving my big sister holding my inside-out shirt, and my little brothers and sisters looking in a mesmerized way.

Free. Free. Free. I run and I dash. Run faster than birds. Through the streets of Dublin ducking in and around people, bouncing off their words. They're saying: 'Catch that boy, he's Oliver Twist, his future education's in deadly risk.' 'Catch that boy, he's the Artful Dodger, he's not been to school, we can tell by the ledger.' 'Catch him quickly lest he grows up a fool, save him from his destiny, the dunce's stool.' But I won't, no I don't, I don't attend school. I broke not the ruler but the strictest rule. Watch, watch me leapfrog over the dunce's stool, and dive head first into a raging whirlpool. Skip over the rope, over the sailor, over the sea. The School Inspector's after me because I'm on the hop. Watch out for the cop. Watch out for the School Inspector's report, watch out for the Probation Officer's report. Watch out for the child psychiatrist's report. For fuck's sake take it easy or you'll never make it to eleven. I will, I will, I will. Stand still. Stand still. I want to examine you. Quiet now while I write my report.

I examined the above boy today, as arranged. He is before the court charged with breaking and entering a toyshop and stealing Dinky toys. His sister states that James is always fighting, both at home with children in the locality and with the children in school: consequently he was put out of his last school. According to the School Inspector's report, though their numbers are low in the school, the headmaster would like to lose James, he cannot make anything of him. In the meantime he is attending no school. He also has a slight stutter, is a nail-biter and is afraid of the dark.

James is a small fair-haired, blue-eyed youth, who is in the average range of intellectual capacity. He admits to being aggressive and to feeling that everyone is against him, and he goes on to comment about his aggressive and delinquent behaviour: 'I can't stop, I do pray and all, but I can't.'

In my opinion this boy is in need of psychiatric treatment at a child guidance clinic before his antisocial behaviour becomes irreversible but I fear James will not attend as an outpatient at a child guidance clinic, so the only solution would appear to be an industrial school for a period of at least two years. This of course will not offer him any real psychotherapeutic treatment but may at least give him a stable environment for a few years.

A report from the Probation and Welfare also states that with such a poor background, James would be better away in an industrial school until he is fourteen years of age. Yours Dr M. Maguire, DPM DCH, Fitzwilliam Square, Dublin 2. Confidential.

The judge in the children's court said I was a goner, that I'd never make it. She told me, You're not wanted in any school, you're not wanted in the child guidance clinic. You're not wanted here – we don't have any facilities for you. The services don't have time for children like you, James. You won't stay still. You come from a dodgy area, you're a dodgy lad. The lockup is the place for your sort. They have the medicine for you, an industrial school, that'll teach you. I'll commit you to an industrial school. I'll put a stamp on that for you. Now, out of my court. Happy birthday James, here's your present, a committal warrant. Now count the steps out: one, two, three, four, five, six, seven, all good children go to Heaven. One, two, three, four, five, six, seven, all bold boys like you go to the Christian Brothers, off you go you little gurrier. They'll stabilize you.

St Joseph's Industrial School, Connemara, Connemara! Maureen O'Hara, Glockamorra. A billion miles from Tara, Land of the Leprechaun, the street urchin, the rainbow, the orphan, the die-hard, eleven-year-old future public enemy number one. Where the Christian Brother with his leather and rubber straps, slaps down from on high the law from the sky, ranting, raving in tormented craving, the words he did utter, you're a child of the gutter, O Lord on high give me this boy and I will make him a man.

Stop, stop, help me they're taking me away. They're dragging me and pushing me and their tight grip hurts me. Stop! Stop, stop this whirlpool, this storm, let me out of here, let me go from here, let me out you bastards. Fuck, fuck, fucking bastards. You will never, never, ever, never, make me cry. Eleven years of age, I think I was. Could have been ten it doesn't matter. Years and years of utter street-urchin laughter ended with the stroke of a pen on a committal warrant to the school for boys. Yes those Brothers, those kind Brothers, I shall never forget them for all they did, they did! They did! They changed my world, upside down and inside out and round and round. I still see them you know, the boys, clearly in my head, those people, those years, you'll never guess what happened.

Home and the family were a long way from West North-West. The boys were my new family and the Brothers, well you can make up your own mind about them. Here goes, stand on your tiptoes between two fingers, hurt and squeeze his snotty, dirty, runny nose, till he grows from a boy to a man with loving slaps of the hand, wham, wham. Bam, bam. One, two, three, four: 'This is the way we started the day, started the day, started the day. This is the way we started the day, on a cold and frosty morning.'

Running around in my head it went never leaving all day, all days, all the time, never changing, except for the day I got out. This was the day I went in. First time, time. Mammy, Mammy, Mammy. Holy God, Holy, Holy … No, no, no, no more mitching on the hop from school, no more ducking and diving, acting the maggot, being the clown fool. No more running down Grafton Street or climbing the roofs of the flats, or huntin' down long dark laneways for dirty big huge rats. Wake me up Mammy, wake me up, I am dreaming about your man Oliver Twist. Wake me up somebody. Where are you? Anybody. Help me, I am falling, falling, felled, held, help, can't, can't get home. Tell me ma, tell me da or me brothers or me sisters that they're killing me and hitting me, bashing me and beating me, slapping me and lashing me in the fields and on the mountains and in the wet cold bogs.

Somebody tell someone. They make us squeal and dance like little pigs. Someone come and get me. Where are you? Where are you? Someone tell someone. Please! Please! Our Father. Hail Mary. Saint Joseph, Saint Jude, Saint, Saint anybody. I fuckin' hate, hate you Saint. No. No I love you, love you. Tell nobody. Shhh. Now, not a word, not a move, not a tear, not a sigh. I'm a man now! Let me go, let me go, let me run. Let me hide away from my memory, remember? It happened! It happened! It happened! Didn't, did, didn't. Did so! No! No! Yes OK. Stop, stop. It's real. It's true, I can face it now, smell the place, almost touch it. Yes, I recognize the school, the home, our home from home. It speaks to me even now, crying, always crying, or is it the wind? Connemara. Connemara. What a winter for a child-boy of eleven.

Listen … do you hear it?

The wind howls, trapped in corners and empty corridors. Listen. There it is. My eyes look around a cracked concrete yard, now overgrown with weeds, where once upon a time, boys, orphans, street urchins, killed time with the aid of a plastic football under the watchful eyes of the Christian Brothers who played their fathers and mothers, armed to the teeth with canes, boots, fists and the hand-stitched leather strap.

And the wind still screams. Stings. My mind is going overboard, straying off down into the depths. Please God, Oh God, help. Merciful God, hold me. I see an army of boys, boys with unspoken names. Boys who will forever wonder who their mothers and fathers were, and why they have been placed in hell's care so early to be starved, beaten and slaved on the nation's land.

The wind stings. It has no knowledge of mercy, and lost boys cannot understand why in the graveyard up at the back, beyond the church and the Brother's monastery, hidden amongst dead wind-twisted rhododendrons, stands a cement cross that carries the names of boys, aged seven, from 1907. Carries the dates of their deaths from past to present. They died of a cold, so we were told, so we were told. Children, children, pray for me, pray, I beg you, for me today as I journey through my childhood steps numbed with the stations of my cross. Unholy memories embrace me while daytime nightmares chase me, whilst the raging wind drinks greedily, mockingly, salt water from my eyes. Oh Connemara, Connemara, Connemara, forever winter and I curse those Christians who called themselves Brothers, whose loving embrace was a slap in the face and the kiss of a leather strap.

The wind rages inside me and all around me, stampeding in panic. I am terrified, please take me away from here. I won't do anything wrong again, never ever, never, cross my heart and hope to die, die, die, die. Jaysus Christ I wish I were dead. Connemara, Connemara, what a winter. Boy ghosts, child ghosts, help me, mind me, be with me. Don't leave me. One, two, three, four, five, six, seven, all good children go to Heaven. My bollix, me bollix.

I will never forget that day, that rainy day in the industrial school toilets, the day I discovered me birdy and me bollix sexually, sex with myself. I was peeing in the little cubical. There wasn't a soul about. Something happened. I'm not quite sure except that it was the first time I would feel them, silky soft, like fluff, smooth as velvet. I dared to look. I was all excited. Something was taking me over as I undid my elastic belt and my short pants dropped to the cold wet jax floor. I could hear my heart jumping and my breathing quicken. 'Please God, don't let the Devil take me nor tempt me,' I whispered under my breath as I turned towards the half-door to get more light. It was at that moment I saw them blonde, silvery blonde, about twenty, maybe more, willy hairs. God saw them too but that didn't matter. This something, this curiosity had me in its grip and it felt wonderful as I stroked and brushed them with my little finger. Then, in an instant, my whole body stiffened. I was frightened and helpless. I wriggled. Butterflies seemed to flutter in me and all around me. I gripped my tiny birdy in my hand. I was lost, tumbling and trembling. The fear of being caught. Everybody catching me. I couldn't stop. I was being carried along, I didn't know why, nor where to. I had never felt this way before. I began to stroke myself. I was racing toward another world. I fought hard to get the image of Holy God and Mary and Joseph out of my head. My birdy stretched and twitched with this strange pleasure, mine, all mine. I vibrated, twisted and turned like never before till I could breathe no more and had to bite my lip to stop me cry-

go back to Connemara. Hooray hooray no more raking hay, no more digging spuds in the mud. Released from St Joseph's Industrial School on medical grounds. Under doctor's care.

The days rolled into days, rolled into days, rolled. Then they put me back in national school, I felt like a dunce, thick and stupid, sitting in a desk too small for me, watching the fleas and the nits go about their daily routine in the mop of hair of your man from Ballyfermot who sat in front of me reefing his head with a wooden ruler. One day I just didn't go. I went to Woolworth's instead and fell in love with the cash register. At night time I didn't go home till late when everyone was asleep. No one to bother me. Freedom, free, free, freedom. Nobody to stop me and the School Inspector and the child psychiatrist were nowhere to be seen, probably gave up on me. My ma would say, 'Oh son, you're for the high jump. They'll take you off me again.' 'No, no, no, Ma they won't. They won't catch me.' But they had, many times, and by the time a year had gone by I was spending more and more time in the children's court listening to the judge read out the charge sheets.

'That you, the said accused, did between the times and the dates, within the Dublin Metropolitan District, did commit the crimes, steal one ladies push-bike, one Batmobile Corgi toy from Woolworth's, one tin of Jacob's assorted biscuits from P.J. Ogden and Co. Did commit malicious damage, did break and enter, rob, steal, thieved, pinched, guilty or not, guilty or not.'

'Yes … no … well kind of.' Thirteen years of age and seventy charges, Jaysus they're going to send me away forever and ever. 'Quiet, silence in court while I listen to the psychiatrist's report and pay attention to me child while I am deciding what to do with you. Stay still.'

I first saw him for the court in 1965 when he was aged

seven. He has been a problem from at least the age of three when he commenced school. He is functioning at the level of dull average intelligence and denies having any problems other than that he might as well continue his life of delinquency as the guards are down on him anyway. He was sent to Letterfrack Industrial School at eleven years and has been home during the past twelve months.

I found him to be a well-nourished boy with a dull manner. His mental age was seven years eight months and his IQ was 68, which places his intelligence at fairly severely mentally handicapped. He could not read or give change and he could only print his name. The boy's mother said that he often takes a bath during the night and remains in the bath for hours and that he is always terrified. Since his return from the industrial school he has had two operations for abdominal obstruction which his mother claims were caused by being kicked while at the school. He has never worked.

He stated that he appeared in court previously for stealing bicycles, stealing from cars and causing malicious damage to a garage. His mother and father stated that he often admits to offences that he has not committed. This boy is certainly a great responsibility. He requires constant supervision and his parents are quite unfit to control him. In my opinion this boy is in need of a period in a unit under the jurisdiction of the court where he could have intensive investigation, treatment and rehabilitation. It is quite certain that he would not attend on an outpatient basis and I fear that residential care at a school for retarded boys would not be a success but a trial would be worthwhile, particularly if sedation were used. Failing that, returning him to an industrial school is the only alternative. Dr M. Maguire, DPM DCH, Fitzwilliam Square, as requested by the Department of Education, Reformatory and Industrial Schools Branch.

'What am I going to do with you. It's me that needs the help. I know, I'll remand you on bail for more psychiatric assessments, physical, mental, emotional and psychological reports, school reports, garda reports. There is something wrong with you, you are the problem. We have nowhere to put you but when we do find a place we are going to lock you up and throw away the key. Can somebody see if there is a vacancy at the reform school? Remand on bail for more reports. See you next week child, if not before. In the meantime be good, be good.'

I will, I will, I will, I will, honest honest, but you're not getting me, I'm leggin' it, having it on my toes, getting offside, doing a bunk, running away, far away, to the big smoke, to England. You caught my two friends but you didn't catch me, do-da, do-da. You caught my two friends but you didn't catch me, do-da, do-da day.

London, London, Big Ben, the big bollix. 'Oh Mother this London's a terrible sight, I'm over here thieving by day and by night.' Tell the truth, you liar, you were over the water two weeks, you never stopped crying, you wouldn't break into a house even if the owner gave you permission but after two weeks, by sheer luck, you managed to rob your fare home. Manky dirty, you arrived back to your ma with an imitation English accent. You gobshite. Two weeks after your travels around the world, you got yourself nicked throwing shapes on the streets with the rest of the corner boys who laughed at you as you were taken off in the squad car. And after pleading guilty to almost seventy charges, half of which you knew nothing about, you got two years in reform school down in the Bog of Allen. Put that in your pipe and smoke it, ya gobshite. Ha ha ha.

Cops, they're mad, stone mad. All the way down to the reform school in the car all they kept saying was: 'Oh be the hokey. Now don't forget to get back to Dublin soon. This road we're on is the way directly to Dublin. Don't forget. Don't forget. Otherwise we'll have feck all to do.'

'Let me out of here,' I kept saying, 'let me out of here.' 'Oh be the hokey, we couldn't do that we'd be sacked, sacked on the spot. We'll never get our promotion.'

At the reform school everybody from the earlier school in Connemara was there, older, harder, tougher. And the Fathers, they were shit scared, we were looking after them! I joined a Dublin gang against the Cork and Limerick gangs. We beat the bollix out of each other. Time sailed by, month after month of nothing to do but sit, sit, sit. Bored, bored, very bored. Turf, turf and more turf. Ah let's have a riot, riot, wreck the kip, smash it up. Ahhhhh. Rip, smash, wreck, rip, burn, tear apart. There's some rocks, there's some poles, break out, break out, smash the windows, bash down the doors, pull down the walls. Reef off the slates, kill, kill, kill, the pain. Mill the cops, but don't, don't, really don't touch the chapel. Father, Son and Holy Ghost. I'm done for now. They're coming, loads of them, they're coming. I'm going to get battered, mashed, left drinking my own blood. No, no, no, no. Bastards, bastards, dirty rotten bastards. My arm. My leg, me head, me head, blackout. Knocked out cold, freezing cold, strait-jacket, straight to the crazy house. Portlaoise.

Dragged to the Portlaoise Hospital where the doctors all said: He can read and write and showed intelligence rather of the cunning, cute evasive type. He has not settled in Daingean and it is unlikely he will do so. In our opinion he shows marked delinquent tendencies with aggressiveness. Because of this he is not a suitable case for St Conleth's Reform School, Daingean. We'd recommend that he receive some treatment in a suitable place where he would be under observation and get the guidance and treatment which would help him to adjust. But not here in this hospital. 'Oh no!' the head chief doctor said. 'You're a nut,' he said, 'beyond the beyond, way outside the pale, my bucko. There is not enough electricity in the whole of Portlaoise to shock you, to stop you, to cure you. You have been a nuisance since you were born and caused havoc since you were three. You need constant supervision and heavy sedation, but not here in my town, not in my county mental hospital. You are a risk to my sanity, you're beyond repair. Better give him back to his parents. I'll sign that, I'll stamp that. I'll authorize that. I'll approve that. We all agree this boy is out of his tree.' Discharged from Portlaoise Hospital on mental grounds by order of the doctor, on behalf of the Oblate Fathers, for the health of the Midlands Health Board.

'I'm mad, am I? I am? You're mad, youse are all mad. I did nothin'. All I did was to hit the Father with a ball of silver paper made from the tops of milk bottles. Doctor, Doctor, Doctor, I didn't start the riot.' I'm not mad, you say. Just bold. Very bold. Terribly bold.

The Fathers, four of them, bundled me into a car, sped to Dublin and dumped me with bus fare. Fourteen years old, not a blade of hair on my shaven head, wired to the moon, dozens of previous convictions, a total no-hoper, in one word, one hundred percent 'doomed'.

And I still feel doomed here today, full of fear at what's to come, what I must face when I go into that courtroom and take the stand. I would love to stop now, have a break. I'd like a recess, a pause and to borrow 65 euro for an inner child looking out counselling session. Anyway looks like the court is about to break for lunch. Justice may be blind but she must be fed.

PART TWO

Seems like I'm the first back, the judge must be eating one of those huge culchie sandwiches. I have the place to meself, ourselves, me and all me memories. You know something, my therapist doesn't do inner child looking out, she only does trauma and aftershock. It took her an hour to tell me that and then she unburdened me of my last 65 euro. I must be the healthiest poorest bastard in this court today. When this is over I'll kill that fucking therapist. Jaysus I wish I was off on one of those Ryanair where are we stranded tours. A destination you can't get back from. It is not to be, have to be present. Stay in the present, feel the feelings I am going through … OK. OK. Don't push. I'm remembering. I remember one hundred percent 'doomed'.

An unruly youth, totally out to lunch. No one at home, wakey wakey! Anyone in? You're in for it now me bucko. Just wait. Have your last fling now and make it last, because it is your last. You're going on your holidays, long holidays; nice walls, nice food, nice clothes, nice bars, lovely cells, unbreakable furniture. Don't rush, you have all the time in the world. Enjoy it while you can son, your time is running out. But Time, real time, is coming. Watch out, your wings are about to be clipped. And they were.

One night, walking home, happy, feeling easy, no real care in the world. It happened. God, do you hear me? You're a weird one, you, you set me up that night, framed me, stitched me, done me in the wrong. Why? Why? Do you remember? I was fifteen and a half, you were ancient and sussed with experience. Was I your guinea pig that night? Your innocent lamb to the slaughter? Suffer little children to come unto me, well where's your Kingdom of Heaven now? Fifteen and every cop in the country screaming for my blood. Blood. Do you remember that night, the street near where I lived? You Bastard. Let me remind you. I was walking home after being with me girlfriend. Remember?

It was about three at night. It was dark and warm. May 1973, does that ring a bell? There was nothing on my mind except sleep. Everything was as it always was as I turned into the street, rested, at one, quiet. Then all of a sudden the whole fucking place erupted. Fire. And I'm in that street, the wrong street at the wrong time, the police grabbing me, dragging me, pushing me, shoving me, down down into their squad car. And you watching, knowing I had nothing to do with it. Do you remember, God, do you remember?

You let them certify me insane. The Criminal Lunatic Act 1838. Section 2 and Central Asylum Act 1845. Medical Certificate. Having examined James X, a prisoner, we hereby certify that he has become insane and are of the opinion that his case may be considered as likely to derive benefit from being placed in the Central Mental Hospital for the criminally insane. You could have stopped them.

The Central Mental Hospital. Largactyl for breakfast, dinner and tea. Liquid lobotomy, zombied. I cannot move my hands, my eyes, cannot sit up cannot nod. Does anybody see me here, over here? Please look into my eyes, I am in here, let me out. Take the wires out of my head. What? I'm not mad doctor, you're only testing? Yes, doctor, that is a picture of an elephant, that one is a car and the other one could be an elephant or a car but I think it is a trick. I think you are trying to trick me. Terrify the life out of me, hold me here forever.

What's that, doctor? I'm only under observation for my own good. I'm difficult and troublesome and I need psychiatric treatment. But there's nothing wrong with me. I told you before it's an elephant. No I don't think it is something else. Well if you think it's a seagull what are you asking me for? I'm not getting aggressive! OK, doctor, it is a seagull. I see a flock of seagulls flying freely through the sky towards the open, the wide open sea. Free as birds flying home to their mammies and daddies, flying home from fucking bird school to get their dinner and there's a big white elephant flying right beside them. Let me out of here please. Please. What, you're letting me go now, is that what you're telling me? I'm fit to stand trial. I'm not insane I'm just part of a subculture. Then what am I doing here in this crazy place? Oh God, is this ever going to end?

'Oh you're guilty,' the judge in the Circuit Court said: 'You're a danger to yourself and the public. Just look at the long list of antisocial behaviour and your previous convictions. You have been in every institution in the country, every mental hospital. There isn't a psychiatrist the length and breadth of the country that doesn't know you. What's the system going to do with you? I have reports going back years that state your possible delinquencies are of a such a serious nature that they recommend full psychological and physical assessments to be done under circumstances of maximum security. And that is from The Children's Hospital! The Probation Services report that you are barred from every industrial school and reform school in the country, that the doctors had to throw you out of St Conleth's Daingean. The doctors from the Central Mental Hospital recently cured you of insanity, but they write here that you are a disturbed boy and in need of psychiatric help. Aren't we all. Aren't we all. I need help. It goes on and on. Another report states that you have a history of head injury in early childhood: had treatment in a child guidance clinic until recent months and that you showed bizarre features in an interview including delusional ideas of influence, "possession and control by little men"; convulsive tics during the interview accompanied by pallor and trembling; homicidal fantasies with elaboration and suggestions of early implementation. Well not here in my court. You're institutionalized. So I'm sending you to St Patrick's institution for a few years. You wouldn't go to school, so I'm sending you to prison. Bye-bye. Slán and happy sixteenth birthday.'

The prison, ah yes, the prison. Years and years of jingle jangle on me ould triangle, jingle, jangle. It's a wonder there's anything left of it. And the ould triangle went jingle jangle. How many years one, two, three, four, how many hours, days, nights, weeks, months in this dirty filthy prison. Time, day after day the same. The same faces I saw way back in Goldenbridge, at Connemara, and in the reform school. The same, the same, the same, the same. Then one night while in my cell, everything became unreal to me. My hands seemed awkward. My legs, my feet, my face, my nose, ears, eyes, the cell, the prison. I became frightened, stiff. My heart pounded in my chest. Nothing like this had ever happened before. My mind raced with paranoia, something was leaving me, everything was leaving me and I was helpless to stop it. I was becoming conscious for the first time of what had happened to me back then when I was eleven and what was happening now: this prison, this cell, me, this body, that world there beyond the walls. Everything I had taken for granted collapsed. Nothing made sense anymore, reason was gone.

I was totally alone. For months and months, I couldn't look at anybody, they all seemed so odd and strange, like as if I was alive in the underworld with the demented. And on visits from my family I just stared at them, at their faces, their hair, their expressions. I could feel no contact with them or anything. Food did not taste. There were no smells, no sense of touch, no feeling anymore. They have driven me insane, I thought, and could tell nobody, ask nobody for help. I was terrified. I walked like a zombie. Now I really was in a nightmare world. I was infested with deadness and going down, down, down and away from myself. I cried for something to earth me, something solid, 'Please God, I'll do anything, just give me back me.'

I lay on my bunk, my eyes looking on to the ceiling. My mind away from my body, distant, a great distance from everything. I stood outside myself, kicking, screaming to get in, back in. The Devil, I thought one night, the dark one wants me. God is a bollix. I was drowning every time I swam against the tide. Now I gave up and let my mind drift down, down into the depths, down into an orgy of madness. I looked at the crucifix that hung on the cell wall and imagined fucking Jesus. I thought of Satan and became alive with power, the power of destruction, destroy, smash, rip apart, the orgy, real or unreal, had begun in my heart, my frightened pumping heart. I wanted life and fun and light but for now the orgy had begun and it possessed me and there was nothing else to do. For months and months I perverted my tormented self and injured it. My mind began to throw up images of me in the thick of fucking all that was supposed to be good – family, friends, faces that meant nothing to me anymore. The images came faster than film. Nothing was sacred, nothing was spared.

This was a new and dangerous world, my world, away from the maddening crowd, away from law and order, the Governor, the outside world. To them, we were only animals savaging each other with no hope of another dimension. And all around me, cells, boxes filled with screaming, howling, prisoners, prowling up and down their cages, raging, raging, raging. And so was I. A no-lifer, no-hoper, banished from the table of food, my spirit was gone. I wanted now, raving, to smash and decimate my soul with thoughts and imaginations of pure corruption. I became nothing, attached to no-one. Crosses were turned upside down and burnt. Holy water was pissed in; communion was shat on; priests and nuns gladly, gladly were cursed most foul. I fucked with Satan and stoked up the heathen fires of hell. In this hell my imagination knew no bounds. This was escape at last and I fell in love with my cell where I could indulge and practice in the dead of night. When the prison, half-awake, half-asleep, got an uneasy rest, I stalked my cell, naked, calling on Satan and cursing you all and damning myself. My God, I did that, it's part of me. Who the fuck am I? What am I? What have I become, what have I done to myself? I cried and cried for days on end. Nobody saw me, nobody guessed that I wasn't the same old me, except me. Soon the Satan fella became a bore, as mundane as the prison regime. God and the Devil had done a runner on me. No more life-rafts. You're on your own now, kid, it's sink or swim or the life of the dead man's float. Floating. Floating. Floating.

In a dream one night, I remember it as clear as water. In the dream I was standing on a star billions of miles away. I was looking, searching for Earth, for me. I looked hard till I found a point, the tiniest little speck. Closer, closer still till I could see

43

Ireland so small, minute. I searched till I came across Dublin, smaller still, then the prison, teeny weeny prison, so insignificant. Then my cell. And I could see me looking out through the bars and I could see me seeing me. And I could see the world around me, all its laws, its prisons, all its wrongs, all its pain, its drudgery, its heartbreak, its grid system, corrals, herds, nations of people. See the sorrow in the prisoners' eyes, the sadness in their walk, their hearts heavy with not a hope in hell and my heart pumped and pumped and went out to them and to me and to all of us. Love, I thought in my dream, love and compassion. Love is the only thing, not madness and destruction. Every one of us is lost, adrift in the one boat, floating, spinning around and around on this our earth, our home. Come love, just love. See the lot of it for what it is. No more wild boy lost in the streets, lost to yourself, lost in the world.

When I woke up that night in the cell I stood on top of my bunk and stared at the dark necklaced night of pearls, diamonds and sapphires, sparkling till dawn. Then the sun broke, beams of light danced across the streets and the rooftops and across the prison yard until it engulfed the whole of Dublin, and later that month the gates closed behind me, doing time was no more. All I possessed were a few belongings, photos, letters. I stepped outside of the prison, I embraced my mother and walked. I didn't want to get a bus, they looked too frightening. Me and my mother walked down the North Circular Road, my heart full of sadness on leaving so many I had got to know behind the walls. Yet my heart was full of hope. Love, I thought, would get me through. It was the only thing. I remember now my mother turning to me, 'Son,' she said, 'it's all over. You're a man now.' And I cried at what had happened.

Free, free, free, twenty years old and free. Copped on and

sussed. Been through it. Done it, survived it. Came out on top. No visible scars, a miracle, a wonder in itself. Society paid in full. One pound of flesh, fresh taken from every part of me. Ah, but sure it will grow again, you're only twenty, take your place now in society and make yourself useful. Give us your contribution.

Wandering the streets of Dublin, looking at old faces, old houses, old mates, expecting a change, but nothing. Everything the same as it ever was, maybe worse. Watching, observing, learning, questioning. Everyone was still in the same place. Maybe some a little older, some dead. And the cops, some now sergeants, some inspectors, superintendent, chief superintendent, super cops, Columbos, Rambos, Dumbos. 'Be the hokey you're looking well. The few years didn't do you any harm,' they said, their mallet heads sticking out the windows of the squad car. 'You learned your lesson, did ye?'

'The only thing I learned in prison,' I replied, 'was the guitar and I taught that to myself, leave me alone. Go play with your promotion. You're getting no more overtime off of me.'

The first week out of prison, four-star hotel treatment. Do you want your dinner in bed? Do you want a new pair of shoes, a jumper, a nice jacket? Do you want a pint in bed? Money? Five? Ten? Twenty? What's wrong with you? Are you alright? Do you want a sambo? Mother was as good and as mad crazy as ever. The rest of the family were grown-up and out scraping an existence. I lazed around. Then one morning it came to an end. My mother in one of her tempers burst in the bedroom door.

'Get up out of that bed you louser and get a job. I'm not keeping you. Come on, up, up, up, up!' Fuck this, give me the prison any day. I was up and out walking about. Looking, searching, scouring Dublin. For what I did not know, any-

45

thing. Shovelling shit would have done, to get me mother off me back, but nothing doing. 'Where did you work last?' the personnel manager asked. 'The log yard of Mountjoy Prison,' my reply. All he was short of doing for my benefit was hitting the panic button.

So I went and asked the Probation and Welfare for assistance and they sent me to a clinical psychologist at the Dept of Justice who gave me the Differential Aptitude Test. The test showed I had a clear lack of aptitude for all school, mechanical and engineering jobs. There is only one area where James shows a reasonable amount of ability and that is clerical aptitude but even here he is below the average level for his age. Consequently, the only type of work that is suitable for James is some fairly routine job that demands some clerical skills. Work of this kind would be typified by routine filling of shelves in wholesale stores, checking labels, matching prices, etc.

Back at the Probation and Welfare office there was a meeting and it was decided that the best hope of a job for me would be in the field of entertainment in pubs or alternatively working on a ship at sea. So I was to take my guitar and fuck off to sea, some rehabilitation! I was once mad bad deranged severely mentally handicapped, a disturbed unruly child, but now I'm captain of my own ship, the Singing Captain, Popeye, Captain Birdseye. Made in Ireland, compliments of the Probation and Welfare, the Church, the Brothers and the nuns, the doctors and the psychologists, the new and improved James X. I was just out of prison wandering around the streets. Roaming around inside myself. I didn't know who I was or what I was, I felt like prey.

Johnny Rotten was on the telly trying to saw his own head off. In St Stephen's Green blokes and girls were going around with nappy pins sticking out of their faces, chains around their necks. I was just wandering around gawking at them, thinking about me time in the Central Mental Hospital for the insane, wondering whether I was still in there or not. I thought I was getting flashbacks from the Largactyl.

Anyway I was twenty and free so I started singing, me and my guitar in the pubs around Dublin – Sheehans, Hogans, Major Toms, the Swan, Keavneys, the Bailey, Falveys, Neary's, Kehoes. I was singing 'God Save Ireland', punk-style. It was the first time I got barred from a pub. So I took to singing on Grafton Street, it was around that time that I met them, me future. I fell in with this band: no, not an armed band with balaclavas. This band wore tights and their ma's dresses over their combats. They called themselves The Lawless. They used to play at the top of Grafton Street 1976-7. I joined them, we were known back then for our ability to empty a street. We were brutal, the only ones that liked us were the cops in Pearse Street, said we were great for public order as there was never a soul about when we played. But I soon changed all that. I changed the band's fortunes and me own. I renamed the band Malicious Damage and we recorded a single on the Split Lip label. The single was called 'Loitering with Intent'. We played it live one Saturday outside the Shelburntout Hotel and we all got nicked for breach of the peace. The judge in the court told the other members of the band to stay away from me, that I was a bad influence on them. Outside the court some of the band's ma's and da's offered me money to stay away from their sons.

After that court appearance everybody wanted to see us and we got a gig in the Frozen Arts Centre. The arty farty crowd came. The theatre crowd, actors, dancers, painters, mime folk. People who do clowning. The Theatre of Butchery, the Theatre of Cruelty. Writers they came and film-makers. They loved us, they couldn't get enough of us. They were all there. The to be's or not to be's, has beens, lesbians, gays, straights, transexuals, the virgin prunes, the musos, the jazzers, the punks, looney tunes, nuts, fruits, commies, swingers and some right wingers. 'All the world's a stage man, and we are merely musicians, know what I mean.' Bono said that to me backstage at my very first staged gig that night at the Frozen Arts Centre. So hi diddle dee dee, it's an artist's life for me. There's no business like show business. There's no business I know. Everything about it is a feeling, everything about it is so gay.

We're on, I am on. Come on, let's let them have it. They're screaming for us, let's give them something to scream about. They'll be screaming all the way to their parents by the time I've finished with them and their student fucking cards. Go home to your mammies or one of your daddies. Are you ready to rock. Rock the system, rock this Frozen Arts Centre, this poncy middle of the middle of the road, middle class's centre. One, two, three, four: Suffer little children to come unto me for theirs is the Kingdom of Heaven. Suffer little children to come unto me for theirs is the Kingdom of the Lord. Suffer Suffer Suffer little children. Suffer little children to come unto me for theirs is the Kingdom of Heaven. Suffer little children to come unto me for theirs is the Kingdom of the Lord. Suffer Suffer Suffer little children to come unto me for theirs is the Kingdom of the Lord, Kingdom of the Lord, of the Lord.

They're lapping it up, come on let's give it to them. Let's smash up the guitars. What? Your daddy bought it for you! So fucking what! I can't do what? Just watch me! We're supposed to be Malicious Damage but you lot are nothing but a bunch of poncy wankers. You what? You're sacking me! But it's my fucking band, I wrote the songs. What does that mean, I'm not compatible. So is that it then? You're legging it, abandoning the band. Running off with my songs. I don't need youse, I'll go it alone, I'll reform, rearm, reload, rename. I'll call myself Malicious Rumour. You're saying I'm an unruly rocker off my rocker, mad and bad and dangerous to know. Don't gig with me that I'm unreliable, unhinged. That I won't turn up. I could have been a contender but you bastards drove me to the bartender.

Look here I am, no hands cuffed. Are you frightened? Are youse frightened? Here I am, a big scary monster. From the cage to the stage, watching you watchin' me. I hear your breathing. I see your faces, that look, that wanting, that waiting for something to happen, a change, a rehabilitation. I could have been a rock star but the fuckers sacked me. Dismissed me. What a build-up, what a let-down, the hills are alive with the Sound of Screaming. I am Screaming in the Rain, just Screaming in the Rain, just raging with the pain. Looking back to where I don't want to look, at me. Must get away from me.

Fuck this. I need an escape, a drink, a drug, a drug, a drink. Mrs Guinness, Mrs Guinness, is Arthur coming out to play? Oblivion. Lets play oblivion. Mission Impossible. This person will self destruct in sixty seconds. Pain zooming in at three o'clock. Low self-esteem nine o'clock. We've got an unidentified feeling heading my way. Self-hatred. Watch out! Abandonment rejection process coming in at six o'clock. This is Memory, Leader. Code name remember, remember. Engaging. Locked on. Dogfight, dogfight. I am in a dogfight. Don't need no bulletproof vest, need 100 per cent proof alcohol. Do you read? Over. Do you copy? Over. Don't leave me on my own, don't abandon me, do you hear me? Need refueling in midair. Flying tanker, high grade intoxicating liquor. Need refuelling. Need refuelling on the 12th parallel. Paralytic on the 12th parallel. This is a no-fly zone. No flies on me.

Over. It's all over, it's nearly all over. All systems go. We have a green light, missiles have launched. Two, I repeat, two low self-esteemers coming in at twelve o'clock, take evasive action, over. Real feelings are about to impact. Take cover incoming. All dysfunctional systems now operational we have full euphoric recall, do you read, a euphoric relapse in progress. Flashback, feedback, playback all dysfunctional systems triggered. Euphoric recall in full progress. Stand back, downloading past images. Feeding in viruses now.

Alcoholic relapse, drug relapse, emotional regression in situ. Stand back, all systems reaching 100 per cent dysfunctional level and triggering, we have activated full addictive compulsion. Dysfunction functional. False self has activated. Full unmanageability in progress. Full powerlessness in situ. Self will run riot any moment now. Countdown. All systems go, five, four, three, two, one. Control, we have out of control, control. Enact, recall, playback. We got some turbulence. I think it's a painful feeling. Have two interceptors ready to fire, two large Paddys with ice. Fire one, fire two, now fuck off feelings, fuck off pain, we have a direct hit. I am numb. No past, no present, no future. Warning signals beep, beep beep, must remember my mission. This is a reclaiming mission. Have to face this. Have to face me.

Drunk I was, for twenty years – out of my head, off my trolley, twisted, stupefied, mankey, mindless, helpless, powerless, mad mad mad. I became a liar, a thief, I did not care. I knew that somewhere, sometime I would go crashing to the wall. I wanted to hurt myself. The prison, the institutions were places that I wished to go back to. There in those dark twisted holes I could find a strange peace. I knew who I was there, what was expected of me, how to survive. I was good at that. The edge was a place I knew very well and alcohol was the fuel that got me there, to the edge of the edge, over the edge. One moment I loved, the next I wanted to destroy. In between I was a falcon who hobbled along a white-striped tarmac landscape, dripping blood from smashed wings, in search of a dark deep cave to bury my sorrow in. Twenty years of lunacy, reacting against everything. Full of anger, anger against me myself. Anger and self-hatred, I cut myself up sometimes, many times, on my legs, my chest, my back, my face, went out of my way for madness.

In and out of the courts I was for Drunk and Disorderly, Simple Drunk, penalty £2 fine. Drunk and Breach of the Peace, £20 fine. Drunk and Loitering with Intent, Drunk and Unlawful Assault. Simple Drunk. Just Drunk. Drunk. A danger while under the influence. Malicious damage to myself, to anything in my flight path. Stand clear! And always angry. I threw it all away, threw my family away, my friends, my career. I could have been a contender but I fell in love with the bartender. I could have been a rock star, but I hit rock bottom.

I was a songwriter written off. Everybody had me written off. Even I had me written off. That's what it was about all the time I wanted to die. It really wasn't about the drunks, the fights, the wreckage. The truth was that, as a going human concern, I didn't matter, not to them and not to me. It has taken me all this time to see it and now here I am again back in court. It's a motherfucker. Is it ever going to end?

I know all these judges, coppers, solicitors and barristers. I know that prisoner, that man over there handcuffed to the prison officer. He's never gotten out of prison, never got out of the system. I met him in the industrial school, now he's doing life for murder. We are all doing life. Most of the kids I met back then are dead or sick with heroin and alcohol. How did it happen? I asked my therapist today why it all happened and why it is still happening to me. She said all I was doing was repeating and all that I had to do was stop repeating. She said I was only as sick as my secrets but that the truth would set me free. To be honest. To honour myself, to let it go. Reclaim myself.

So here goes. See that story I've just told you. That's the same story I told to myself all my life. That's my grandiose story, my euphoric recalling of the events of my life. If I hadn't got that version I wouldn't have survived. You see I didn't discover my birdy myself at the industrial school. No, no, no, it did not happen like that. That's false. That's my sideshow story, my Jewish humour. But now it's time to tell the truth. The honest truth. This is my statement. My truth. The real story. The story I came to tell.

My name is James O'Neill. I was born on 14 May 1957.

When I was eleven years of age I got sent away to the industrial school. I think it was for not going to school and robbing toy cars. On the day I arrived the Brother who drove me from the station orally raped me in the car. On another occasion during my time at the school, the caretaker came to my bed at night and took me into the toilets. I was half-asleep and didn't know what to do. He threatened me and held me by the hair. He held his hand over my mouth and he anally raped me.

Another time I was with a few other boys, we were hungry, we stole some communion wafers from the church sacristy. I was caught by a Brother who kicked me in the stomach until I vomited up the wafers. When I got holidays that summer, I had to have an operation as a result of that beating. I still have a huge scar on my stomach.

Another time in the dining-hall after everybody had gone another Brother approached me. He asked me whose boy I was, I told him that I was my mother's boy. He ripped at my clothes. I tried to get away but he grabbed me and kissed me, he kept kissing me. I broke away from him and ran away from the school but I was caught. Later that night in the dormitory this same Brother brought me to his room at the end of the dormitory, stripped me of my pyjamas and lashed me for an hour. I was sick and ill for weeks after the beating. I still have scars on my body. I spent almost a year and a half at the industrial school. I never told anybody what happened in these places, especially this one.

Later on, when I was about thirteen and a half, I got sent to the reformatory school for older boys for two years. There it was much the same. Every time you didn't do what they wanted you to do, the Fathers beat you. All I ever got was clatters and kicks. The Fathers said I was stupid. They put me cleaning the lavatories. Some of them called me Ajax.

At fifteen the courts sent me to prison. During that time I was physically and sexually abused by another prisoner in my cell. I complained but nothing happened.

Then one day I was handcuffed and taken to the hospital for the criminally insane. I can't describe how horrific and how terrifying that place was. Nobody would tell me why I was there and I feared I was doomed to stay there forever. All through my detention I lived with the threat, the mental anguish, and the nightmare of being sent back to that very sick place. All my life I have lived with the wrongs that were done to me. When I tried to tell people what happened in my childhood years, nobody wanted to know what happened to me and to the other people sent to those places. Nobody trusted us and nobody cared, we were all abandoned. Today all I ask is that you believe me. That justice be done.

I never spoke those words till now, never had the voice, only the fear. I thought it was all my fault. I felt it was my fault and drinking my bollix off numbed the pain away. Until it became too much to take and now here I am back in your court, clean and sober and just about to throw myself at the mercy of the very system that I have been up against all my life. But not today. Today I will not let go my hand.

They are calling my name now to take the stand. Funny, it is just the same way they called it out back at the children's court in Dublin Castle all those years ago. If I walk into that courtroom now I'll never again walk back into my own life. They'll give me the few bob, their financial redress, and push me back out on to the street. Plead Guilty and Sons want me to take a no-fault settlement – that's like pleading guilty to something I didn't do – right up their street!

But not today, all I am here for now is to hand them back this file and give them my statement. This is what was done to me when I was helpless, when I had no voice, no one to turn to. When I was a child. This is not my shame anymore, it never was. I've carried it long enough. It is yours and today I am giving it back. So here's your file, File No. 195702, your words, property of the State, the Church, their servants and agents and you the citizens. And this statement, this is your shame. There is no care in this file, no love.

FILE NO: 195702

NOT TO BE READ IN OPEN COURT

ÉIRE **IRELAND**

Uimhir
Number **V** № **8687**

57

. DEIMHNIÚ BREITHE
BIRTH CERTIFICATE
Na hAchtanna um Chlárú Breitheanna agus Básanna 1863 go 1972
BIRTHS AND DEATHS REGISTRATION ACTS 1863 to 1972

Ainm agus Sloine
Name and Surname . *James X.*

Gnéas.
Sex. *Male*

Lá
Day. *Fourteenth*

Dáta Breithe}
Date of Birth}

Mí.
Month. *May*

Bliain
Year. *1957*

Mile
One Thousand. *Nine*

gCéad
Hundred and. *Fifty seven*

Ceantar Cláraitheachta
District of Registration *Coombe Hospital*

í gContae
in the County of ... *Dublin*

Éire
Ireland

Uimhir an Taifid
Number of Entry. *6*

Deimhnim le seo gur thiomsaíodh na sonraí thuasluaithe ó Chlár-leabhar na mBreitheanna atá faoi mo chúram.

I hereby certify that the foregoing particulars have been compiled from a Register of Births in my custody.

Oifig
Office. SUPT. REGISTRAR'S OFFICE

Dáta
Date. JOYCE HOUSE 8-11 LOMBARD ST. E.

Cláraitheoir *(Maoirseachta)
†(Superintendent) Registrar

*Scrios amach an focal (idir lúibíní) mura n-oireann sé. †Strike out words in brackets if not applicable.

Is cion trom é an teastas seo a athrú nó é a úsáid taréis a athraithe

TO ALTER THIS DOCUMENT OR TO UTTER IT SO ALTERED IS A SERIOUS OFFENCE

CONGREGATION OF THE SISTERS OF MERCY
South Central Province

Mercy

To Whom It May Concern:

This statement confirms that the following information is recorded in the Mercy Congregational Archives:

James X of 2 Connolly House, Dublin, was in St Vincent's Industrial School, Golden Bridge, Inchicore, Dublin in 1964.

Signed:

Sr. Maura O'Reilly
Provincial Leader.

Mercy
Congregational
Archives

| James X | 2 Connolly House | 25. 6. 64 | 9. 7. 64 |

57

DUBLIN CORPORATION
BARDAS ÁTHA CLIATH
School Attendance Committee
Register of legal proceedings at the Children's Court, Dublin Castle, for non-attendance at school.

Date: 12th January 1965

Plaintiff: R.O'Brien

Child: James X

Address: 2 Connolly House, Dublin

Age: 7yrs 8 mths

Justice: D.J. Prendergast

Fine: --

Costs: --

Remarks: Adj. To 12th Fevruary 65 @ 2.30

Date: 12th February 1965

Plaintiff: R.O'Brien

Child: James X

Address: 2 Connolly House, Dublin

Age: 7yrs 9mths

Justice: Miss Kiely

Fine: --

Costs: --

Remarks: Probation Act

58

Freagraí chuig
Oifigeach Promhaidh

Replies to
Probation Officer

Teileafón 776831 Ext 10

AN tSEIRBHIS PHROMHAIDH
(The Probation Service)

5 CAISLEAN ATHA CLIATH
(5 Dublin Castle)

ATH CLIATH 2
(Dublin 2)

JAMES X, 7½ yrs
2 Connolly House, Dublin.

CHARGE: Pearse St. J48. Larceny cash £3.2.5

This boy is not attending any school at present. On account of his conduct the teacher at his last school was unable to keep him and the head teacher of another local school will not accept him.

PARENTS: Father, Liam, works as a labourer and contributes about £8. per week. Mother, Kathleen, housekeeps.

FAMILY: 11 Children
May 16 yrs, in a sewing factory and contributes £2 per week to the home. Sue 14½ yrs. Not living at home at present. Martina, 13 yrs., Barbara 12 yrs., Angela all all going to school. James, subject of charge.
Anthony 6 ¼ yrs., Brian 5 ¼ yrs., Pauline 3¼ yrs., Christopher 1¼ yrs,. And Johnny 7 months.

HOME: Corporation flat, poorly furnished and fairly clean. Rent 15/-. Per week.

INCOME: About £10 per week at present. Plus children's allowance.

GENERAL: This boy comes from a large family and Mrs X informed me there was also trouble between herself and her husband and he was away from the home for some time. This young lad may need treatment, and a psychiatrist's report will help the court in this matter.

(Mary Leahy)
Probation Officer.

Hours by appointment only   Dr M. Maguire   Fitzwilliam Square
                                                               Dublin

CONFIDENTIAL

17th February 1965

James X - aged 7
Dublin

Born May 1957

    I examined the above boy today. He is charged with
stealing a sum of approximately £2.10.0 while in the company of
another boy. He was accompanied to the interview by his 12 year
old sister, (they arrived on the wrong day and at the wrong
time, only the venue was correct),as his mother was ill and his
father was working. Neither he nor his sister were sure whether
he had been charged previously for stealing from cars.

    He is the 6th in a family of 11 children, both parents
alive, father in constant employment. . . . his sister states
that James is always fighting both at home, with children in the
locality and with the children in school: consequently he was
put out of his last school, and is now waiting to be admitted to
another school on his 8th birthday, but in the meantime he is
attending no school. He also has a slight stutter, is a nail-
biter and is afraid of the dark.

    James is a small fair haired, blue eyed youth, who is in
the average range of intellectual capacity. He admits to being
aggressive and to feeling that everyone is against him, and he
goes on to comment re his aggressive and delinquent behaviour:
'I can't stop, I do pray and all, but I can't.'

    In my opinion this boy is in need of psychiatric treatment
at a Child Guidance Clinic before his antisocial behaviour
pattern becomes irreversible. . . . The Child Guidance Clinic,
Orwell Road, would be the most suitable clinic for him to
attend, if the Court is agreeable and the probation officer
would arrange an appointment

Dr Maureen Maguire D.P.M.,D.C.H.

60

APPOINTMENT CARD

HOSPITALLER ORDER OF ST. JOHN OF GOD
CHILD GUIDANCE CLINIC

59 ORWELL ROAD, RATHGAR, DUBLIN 6   Telephone 904696

James X and parent.

Re : ....

....

11.00 a.m

The appointment for the above-named is arranged for....................

Monday October 9th, 1967

on ....

If you cannot keep this appointment, kindly inform Brother Secretary as soon as possible.

A MAN

JAMES X

HOSPITALLER ORDER OF ST. JOHN OF GOD
CHILD GUIDANCE CLINIC
59 ORWELL ROAD, RATHGAR, DUBLIN 6   Telephone 904696

CASE HISTORY

X, James - aged 10
2 Connolly House,
Dublin.

9th October 1967

Developmental History:

The birth was normal; the baby was nine pounds and bottle-fed. He sat at four months, walked at a year, was talking at a year and a half and toilet trained at two. He started school at three but was a problem to the teacher from the start as he was always fighting with other children. From the age of eight years old he had been mitching. He was excluded from school for seven months for aggressive behaviour with other children, he has not been at school at all this term.

When he was first in court two years ago (aged 8), for breaking into an office, he was put on probation and recommended to a Doctor in Harcourt Street Children's Hospital. The next time he was in Court was in August 1966 for climbing onto biscuit factory roof and taking a box of milk chocolates. The Justice again referred him for treatment but the mother did not get an appointment. The third time he is to be in Court for taking the slates off a roof and entering a warehouse from which he stole toy guns and bikes. The mother went to the Police herself about this last offence. . . . The family have not succeeded in getting a house; the thirteen of them share two bedrooms and sleep in bunk beds. . . . an appointment for a test has been arranged for James.

HOSPITALLER ORDER OF ST. JOHN OF GOD
CHILD GUIDANCE CLINIC
59 ORWELL ROAD, RATHGAR, DUBLIN 6   Telephone 904696

CASE NOTES   - James X, 2 Connolly House,Dublin

10th October 1967

James was referred by Miss Carroll, Probation officer, for
investigation of truancy from school. The full history was not
available to me when I saw him, but I understand that he has also
been anti-social in other ways. He was referred here two years
ago and placed on a waiting list but an appointment was not made
for him. He has now been out of school for the greater part of
the past year and seems to spend most of his days wandering about
the streets. . . James is one of 11 children . . . He is a
strongly built lad for ten and looked the typical street waif,
being dressed poorly and having lots of mud spattered over his
arms and legs. He related easily and gave the impression of
being used to adult company and to sensing adult reaction to him.
He obviously only said what would please, at times, and he was
quite evasive concerning his school attendance.

He felt that coming here might save him from the
industrial school but he told me he knew many boys in the
various industrial schools and, wherever he goes, he'd have some
friends. He complained bitterly about the masters in the various
schools and accused them all of having huge poles to beat boys
like himself. He gave dramatic accounts of many of these
episodes and suggested that some of the teachers would be better
off in St John of God Hospital. ... .

He has no ideas for the future and is content to drift
along, taking what is coming to him. He became interested in many
things in my room, wandering over and checking the various toys
and making suitable comments. He obviously enjoys sport and was
able to talk about golf, when he saw a golf stick here, and
cricket, when he saw the cricket bat. He watches television in
the evening time and he appears to be quite a perceptive boy, who
takes in quite a lot from what he sees and hears.

When asked about dreams or nightmares, he said he used to
have them years ago, but not in recent years and he could not
recall any. He sleeps with a brother and said he sleeps well.
In general, he gave me the impression of being quite a contented
lad in his own way, and not very concerned about any of his antisocial behaviour. Appointments were made for psychological
testing and for a further interview with me.

HOSPITALLER ORDER OF ST. JOHN OF GOD
CHILD GUIDANCE CLINIC
59 ORWELL ROAD, RATHGAR, DUBLIN 6   Telephone 904696

RECORD OF VOCUBULARY AND COMPREHENSION TEST ON - __JAMES X. AGED 10 ½ - Oct '67__

DONKEY:	Thing you have in a field, like a horse - pulls turf in a small cart.
FUR:	You wrap it round you, fur coat - comes from squirrels.
DIAMOND:	You wear in a ring, a jewel.
JOIN:	Come on.
SPADE:	Dig with.
SWORD:	Fight with - stick in people - kill people with.
STOMOAH:	Makes you eat.
NUISANCE:	Fellow that keeps annoying you.
BRAVE:	In war if you stand up to a 100 men.
NONSENSE:	If you're fighting a fellow
HERO:	Brave man - fellow who's fighting and killing everyone.
GAMBLE:	A toss club - throwing your money away.
MICROSOOPE:	Thing you talk through.
FIGHT:	Get a fellow small enough for you.
CRIMINALS:	If you ever let them out you don't know what they'll do.
OHARITY:	People might drink with it.
PROMISE:	It's a promise it's wrong to break it.
CAT / MOUSE:	They both got tails.

64

CONFIDENTIAL

8th May 1968

James X - aged 10,
2 Connolly House,
C/o Place of Detention, Marlborough House, Dublin.

Born: 14. 5. 57

I examined the above boy today, as arranged. He is
before the Court charged with breaking and entering a toyshop
and stealing Dinky toys. He tells me that he has been in
Court on at least seven previous occasions since the age of
eight. The list of his delinquencies were long and numerous
. . . He is the 6th in a family of 14 children, both parents
alive - father works as a labourer . . .

Apparently, James was referred to the Child Guidance
Clinic Orwell Road two years ago, but did not keep an
appointment. He did, however, attend in October of 1967,
when he was found to be in the average range of intellectual
ability but completely retarded scholastically. In spite of
being given a couple of appointments and there having been
five home visits, James did not attend any further.

I found him to be a small, fair haired, blue eyed boy,
with badly bitten nails, but quite well dressed. He told me
that he had been a patient in Harcourt Street Children's
Hospital with blackouts. When I checked there, I found that
nothing organic had been found and it was concluded that
there was nothing of serious significance in them. James can
give no explanation of his delinquency but thinks "I should
be sent away because she gave me a good few chances.". . . .

James will not attend as an outpatient at a Child
Guidance Clinic, and as we have no residential facilities for
such children, the only solution would appear to be an
industrial school for a period of at least two years. This,
of course, will not offer him any real psychotherapeutic
treatment but may at least give him a stable environment for
a few years.

M. MAGUIRE, DPM, DCH

65

AN tSEIRBHIS PHROMHAIDH
(The Probation Service)

5 CAISLEAN ÁTHA CLIATH
(5 Dublin Castle)

ÁTH CLIATH 2
(Dublin 2)

I   **PROBATION OFFICERS REPORT**

Court ____ Metropolitan Children's Court ____ Date. 9.5.68

Name ____ James X

Address ____ 2 Connolly House, Dublin

Date of Birth .14.5.1957

Occupation. Schoolgoing

Religion . RC

James is the 6th in a family of 11 children, he is the eldest
boy and has 3 younger brothers. . . . I spoke to James'
teacher at his national school. He had been put out of a
couple of schools before he started attending his present one
three years ago. The headmaster told me that James is the
most difficult boy in the school, that he can learn and does
make some attempt, also that he is a fairly good attender at
present though he has been before the Court for non-
attendance. But he is a bad influence among the other boys
and often brings articles which have been stolen into the
classroom. The headmaster said that though their numbers are
low in the school, he would like to lose James, that he cannot
make anything of him.

I think that with such a poor background that James would be
better away in an industrial school until he is 14 years of
age.

Evelyn Carroll.

(Evelyn Carroll)
Probation Officer

AN CHÚIRT DÚICHE THE DISTRICT COURT

CHILDREN ACTS, 1908 to 1941 TO 57

ORDER OF DETENTION IN A CERTIFIED INDUSTRIAL SCHOOL

ATTORNEY GENERAL &   *Complainant.*

GARDA POWER   Dublin Metropolitan District.

JAMES X   *Defendant.*

WHEREAS   JAMES X

who appears to the Court to be a child under the age of twelve years (having been born, so far as has been ascertained on the 14th May 1957 and who resides at   2 Connolly House, Dublin in the County Borough of Dublin, has been charged before the Court with the offences of   Larceny   punishable in the case of an adult by   imprisonment & Road Traffic Act

AND WHEREAS the Council of the said County Borough has been given an opportunity of being heard;

AND WHEREAS the Court is satisfied that it is expedient to deal with the said child by sending him to a Certified Industrial School;

AND WHEREAS the religious persuasion of the said child appears to the Court to be Catholic:

IT IS HEREBY ORDERED that the said child be sent to the Certified Industrial School at   St. Joseph's, Letterfrack, Co Galway being a school conducted in accordance with the doctrines of the Catholic Church, the managers whereof are willing to receive him, to be there detained until the 1st day of   July   1970   , commencing from and after this day.

AND IT IS FURTHER ORDERED that

residing at   the parent of the said child shall pay to the Inspector of Reformatory and Industrial Schools a weekly sum of shillings and   pence until further order. First payment on the

Given under my hand at the METROPOLITAN CHILDREN'S COURT, Dublin Castle, the   27th day of June 1968.

Justice of the District Court.

4108-A. 5,000. 10/88, W.R.& S.LTD.—0200.

67

(see 21.)

St. Joseph's CB Industrial School
Letterfrack, co. Galway
19 69

Notice of Discharge, Release on Supervision, Transfer,
Absconding, Hospitalisation and all other
Re-admissions, etc.

[stamp: 2 SEP 1969]

Name and Number	Nature of Movement	Date	Particulars of disposal (wages, employment, etc.)	Has (a) Supervision Certificate been issued; (b) Health Authority been notified (Sec. 3(3) C.A. 1957).
James X 2216	Did not return yet as he is under doctors care.	1-9-69		

AN tSEIRBHIS PHROMHAIDH
(The Probation Service)

5 CAISLEÁN ÁTHA CLIATH
(5 Dublin Castle)

ÁTH CLIATH 2
(Dublin 2)

6/10/1970.

James X.

I phoned Dr. Dunne who is attached to Harcourt St
Children's hospital. He first saw James in 1967 after he had
suffered a black-out. James then went to Letterfrack and he
was not seen again by Dr. Dunne until 1969. He was home from
holidays from Letterfrack and got an attack of dizziness and
was admitted to Harcourt St Hospital. He was again admitted
in Jan. 1970 and again in July 1970. He has spent 4 months
between these dates in England. Epilepsy has been suspected
but not firmly diagnosed. Dr Dunne said that he should be
under regular medical supervision and on medication.

I phoned the Brother who is principal in Letterfrack. He
said that James had not suffered from any blackouts or
attacks while in Letterfrack but while he was home on
holidays in July in 1969 he had abdominal operations
performed at a Dublin Hospital and had not returned to
Letterfrack afterwards. He still complains of abdominal
pains. He was not any trouble while at school in Letterfrack.

I phoned Dr. Kelly who is attached to the Orwell Road
Child Guidance Clinic. He saw James twice in 1967 and there
was psychological testing done. His I.Q. was 86 and he had
good verbal attainments but was unable to read and write.

Evelyn Carroll.
(Probation Officer)

```
                                                    Dr D. McCarthy,
                                                    6 The Heights,
To:    The Clerk of the Juvenile Courts,            Tallaght,
       Dublin Castle                                1.11.'70
```

Re James X, aged 13 years 6 months, 2 Connolly House, Dublin.

Dear Sir,

I examined this boy at his home following his appearance in court on a robbery charge. He comes about the centre of a family of 13, his father is employed and his mother keeps house. . . . He was sent to Letterfrack Industrial School at 11 years and has been home during the past 12 months. Mrs. X stated that he gave considerable trouble there also. Mrs X stated that he takes a bath during the night and remains in the bath for hours and that he is always terrified. Since his return home he had two operations for abdominal obstruction which Mrs.X claims were caused by being kicked while at Letterfrack. He has never worked

I found him to be a well-nourished boy with a dull manner. His mental age was 7 years 8 months and his I.Q. was 68, which places his intelligence at fairly severely mentally handicapped. He could not read or give change and he could only print his name. His vocabulary was at the 8 year level and his comprehension was poor. He however adopted an obstructive attitude and this may be a low reading. He was clean and tidy and his attitude was not in keeping with his low I.Q.

He stated that he appeared in court previously for stealing bicycles, stealing from cars and causing malicious damage to a garage. His mother and father stated that he often admits to offences that he has not committed. In this instance he admitted he took a handbag from a girl in Stephen's Green removed the money and threw away the bag. His father stated that he gave the money to other boys who were with him . . . . This boy is certainly a great responsibility and requires continuous supervision and his parents are quite unfit to control him. It is essential that his medication should be continued.

I fear that residential care at a school for retarded boys would not be a success if close supervision would not be obtained, but a trial would be worthwhile particularly if sedation were used. Failing that returning him to an industrial school is the only alternative.

Yours sincerely,

Denis McCarthy
_____

Dr. David McCarthy M.D. D.P.A.

AN BORD SLAINTE LAR TIRE
OSPIDEAL NAOMH FIONNTAIN PORTLAOISE
GUTAN 21205

MIDLAND HEALTH BOARD
ST. FINTAN'S HOSPITAL, PORTLAOISE
TEL. No. 21205

Daingean House,   27th May 1971
Daingean.
    Re/ James X (14), c/o St Conleth's School, Daingean.

Dear Dr.O'Brien,
I saw the above named boy on 25-5-'71. At interview he appeared
reluctant and resentful at being interviewed stating he did not like
being asked questions about himself and his family. However, he
informed me that he left school at the fifth standard. He then went to
Letterfrack Industrial School for problem children, which he did not
like at all. The brothers were hard on him and did not treat him well.
Following leaving Letterfrack he went back to primary school but did not
continue. He stated that he never attended school regularly and was
continually mitching and admitted to being in trouble for stealing
saying that he thinks that was why he was sent to Letterfrack.

He said he had a job for three to six months as a delivery boy following
leaving school but did not like it as it was far away from his home and
difficult to get to. When I asked him why he was in Daingean he said I
am in Daingean for robbing. I should not be in it as I did not rob.
The police said I did. Since I came to St. Conleth's three months ago I
got on all right. I was not in any trouble, I did not kick or hit
anybody. I am treated fairly well there but I do not want to stay on.

When questioned about his nerves he stated that he felt his mind was
disturbed and that he worried a lot about himself and that he was afraid
of hurting people because of not being able to control his actions. He
was seen by a psychiatrist in the children's hospital, Harcourt Street
years ago and received tablets there. He admitted that he had been in
trouble on and off for a long time and that he did not seem to be able
to control this behaviour.

This boy presented during interview as being a low standard of
education, showing very poor sense of responsibility lacking in control
of his behaviour and rather resentful and aggressive in his manner and
approach. He can read and write and showed intelligence rather of the
cunning, cute and evasive, type. He has not settled down in St.
Conleth's and it is unlikely that he will do so.

In my opinion he shows marked delinquent tendencies with aggressiveness.
Because of this he is not a suitable case for St. Conleth's school.
I would recommend that he receive some treatment in a suitable place
where he would be under observation and get guidance and treatment which
would help him to adjust,
yours sincerely,

J.P. Walsh
(Res Med Supt.)

71

21ˢᵗ July 1971

Private & Confidential
Not to be read in open court

As requested by

The Secretary
The Department of Education,
Reformatory and Industrial Schools Branch
Marlborough Street,
Dublin 1

James X - aged 14
2 Connolly House, Dublin. C/o Marlborough House]

I examined the above boy as requested Mr. Ryan.

The reason for the request was that he had attempted
to escape from Marlborough House, been obstructive, and had put
his hand through the glass window since his admission yesterday.
He is on remand for a week because of being charged with
loitering with intent.

This boy has been a problem from at least the age of
three years, when he commenced school. I first saw him in 1965
for the Court. . . . He spent a period both in Daingean and
Letterfrack.

James, who is a tall, fair haired, blue eyed boy, has
badly bitten nails and cuts on his face and right hand at the
moment. He is functioning at the level of dull average
intelligence. He denies having any problems other than that he
might as well continue his life of delinquency as "the guards are
down on him anyway."

In my opinion, this boy is in need of a period in a
unit under the jurisdiction of the court where he could have
intensive investigation, treatment and rehabilitation. I think
it quite certain that he would not attend on an outpatient basis.
In the absence of such a facility, and as he cannot be contained
in Marlborough House, perhaps a period in Mountjoy might be
considered.

M. Maguire, DPM DCH

72

NATIONAL CHILDREN'S HOSPITAL
HARCOURT STREET
DUBLIN 2

TEL. 752355-6-7-8-9

Re. James X   - aged 15,
C/o St Patricks Institution.   9th May 1973

        I examined the above boy today as requested. He is charged with breaking and entering a hardware store. He has been in Court on many previous occasions and was sent to Daingean he was also sent to Letterfrack at some other period.

        As he is due in Court tomorrow and I only saw him this morning there was no time to see his parents and James himself was a bit confused about his history, for instance he was not even sure of his date of birth, nor did he know how many brothers and sisters he had but thought he had about 14.

        The Welfare Officer Mr McCabe informed me that James is thought to have attended me in Harcourt Street Children's Hospital some years ago. Unfortunately there is no record of that available. However there is a record of his having attended Dr Dunne, the specialist in epilepsy following a head injury in 1970. He has an E.E.G. done at this time which was inconclusive as to the possibility of epilepsy or not but certainly did not outrule it. However he did not attend Dr Dunne after July 1970 and at that time Dr Dunne was not yet apparently satisfied as to whether he had a true epilepsy or not.

        With me today James, who is a tall thin fair haired blue eyed youth, appeared to be co-operative but I did not at all feel that I could believe very much of what he said. . . . . . .

        James denies having broken into the hardware shop and says that he only made a statement that he did so because he was fearful of the guards but does go on to say that they did not touch him but he was afraid that they might. The reason he gives for saying that he would do it again was that he was so "mad with them".

        This boy would appear to have many problems. He is obviously very disturbed, he admits that he never works, that he gets all his money by robbing, there is a possibility the he may have an organic brain lesion such as a form of epilepsy. As his possible delinquencies are of such a serious nature I would advise that this boy be fully investigated physically by a Neurologist, E.G. full psychological assessment etc. but think that this investigation should be done under circumstances of maximum security such as at Dundrum.

Dr. M. Maguire, D.P.M. D.C.H.
        F.R.C. Psy.

AN tSEIRBHIS PHROMHAIDH
(The Probation Service)
5 CAISLEAN ATHA CLIATH
(5 Dublin Castle)
ATH CLIATH 2
(Dublin 2)

Welfare Services,
St Patrick's Institution,

9th May 1973

Name: James X

Born: 14.5.1957

Address: 2 Connolly House, Dublin

Status: Single

Offence: Between 6.00,p.m. on 2.5.1973 - 2.00 a.m on 3.5.1973 feloniously breaking and entering promises and committing a felony.

Parents: Father employed as a labourer. Mother housekeeps. There are 13 children 7 girls and 6 boys.

Home: A small rented corporation flat of 2 bedrooms, a living room and a scullery. The family have lived all their life in Connolly House, which is situated about ½ mile from the city centre. The home was clean but sparsely furnished although they had a T.V. and radiogram in the living room. Altogether inadequate accommodation for the number in the family.

Education:
/Work   James was a pupil at National school but was a bad attender. For criminal offences he was committed to Letterfrack Industrial School where he remained for over a year. Subsequently he was committed to Daingean for two years but was only there for 4 months when the authorities had him returned home as it was considered by a consultant psychiatrist from Portlaoise that he was unsuitable for Daingean. James can read and write which he learned while in Letterfrack. The subject had only one job delivering letters - he remained in this a few months.

General: James parents have no control over him and it is suspected that he is abusing drugs. He also takes alcoholic drink but not excessively. Has not been known to use violence in the home nor has he gone missing from home with the exception of one or two occasions. Both parents were never in court for criminal matters.

This is a deprived family and from my discussions I concluded that parental control has not been exercised, with the result that James has no regard for any lawful authority. I gather that he has been involved in malicious damage on about two previous occasions. I was informed that relationships are good between the subject and the other family members. I noted that while I was present at least two of the younger children disregarded completely instructions given to them by their mother. On the night previous to my visit I noted that the young girl of 12 years had been left in charge of the family from 8.00 p.m. to 9.30 p.m. with no adult present. Mrs X did not provide me with any substantial reason for this when asked.

James attended Dr Maguire, psychiatrist and Dr Dunne Harcourt Children's Hospital. Dr Maguire advised me that Dr Dunne was seeing James in regard to possible attacks of epilepsy but his investigations were not concluded as James did not return.

D. Mangan.
Welfare Officer.

Criminal Lunatic (Ireland) Act 1838 Sec.2 and Central Asylums (Ireland) Act
1845 Sec 12, 8 and 9 Vic c.107

Form P 48.

MEDICAL CERTIFICATE.

In case of an Insane Prisoner (under 1st Vic., c. 27, and 8 & 9 Vic., c. 107)
and Certificate from the Governor of the Prison.

St Patrick's Institution Prison | Having examined *James X*

(73)

now a prisoner in *St. Patrick's Institution*

to wit | under sentence of *3 Months Detention*

we hereby certify that *he* has become insane and we are of opinion that *his*

case may be considered as* *likely to derive benefit from being placed in the Central Mental Hospital*

Given under our hands this *19th* day of *May* 19 73

P.S. Gilmartin Medical Doctor

B.R. W Medical Doctor

St. Patrick's Institution Prison

I hereby certify that the above-named prisoner, Reg. No. *4179/73*, whose

particulars are given below, is now in my custody.

Martin O'Reilly Governor.

19th day of *May* 19. 73

PARTICULARS OF THE ABOVE-NAMED PRISONER.

Crime, *Larceny of purse value 50p and £15 cash.*

Date of Conviction, *15.5.73*

Sentence, *3 Months Detention.*

Date of termination of sentence, *14.8.73*

Earliest possible date of release } *22.7.73*
on remission of sentence

Where Convicted, *Dublin Children's Court*

By whom Committed, *———*

Age on Conviction, *16 years.*

County and place of Birth *Dublin*

CENTRAL MENTAL HOSPITAL NIGHT BOOK ENTRIES FOR JAMES X.
Admitted to the Central mental Hospital on the 21st May 1973 and
discharged on the 1st June 1973.

21st May 1973

New patients admitted: James X from St. Patricks Institution to
ward 1A. The newly admitted patient James X, took two
tablespoons of largactil syrup and slept well.
Dr. Martin visited the sick and James X at 9.30pm.

22nd May 1973
No entries for James X.

23rd May 1973
James X .... Slept well without a sedative

24th May 1973
James X .... Slept well without a sedative

25th May 1973
Removed and to where: ...... James X to ward 1B from 1A
Slept well without a sedative

26th May 1973
James X .... Slept well without a sedative

27th May 1973
James X .... Slept well without a sedative

28th May 1973
No entries for James X.

29th May 1973
No entries for James X.

30th May 1973
James X ...... Slept well without a sedative

31st May 1973
James X .... Slept well without a sedative

1st June 1973
Removed and where to: James X to St Patricks Institution from 1B

_____
Area Manager

Martin Malone
Clinical Director

76

Bord Sláinte an Oirthir
P: 'h Ospidéal Meabhairgalar
Dun Droma
Átha Cliath 14

Eastern Health Board
Central Mental Hospital
Dundrum
Dublin 14

Tel 98 43 28
Your ref
Our ref

1st June, 1973

Dear Dr Stevens,

Re: James X

I interviewed James on 30/5/1973. Because of
the short time available it is possible only
to offer a preliminary report.

W.A.I.S. (Weschler Adult Intelligence Scale)
The verbal I.Q. 96 and performance I.Q. 92 yielded
a fullscale I.Q of 94 representing intellectual
functioning during the interview to be within the
normal range.

M.M.P.I.
The profile indicates strong asocial identification
with rather withdrawn features and a severe distrust
of others. The profile indicates a high level of
tension. The test was not faked. The lie scale is
within the normal range. There is no evidence of a
psychotic process.

Hoping that my findings will be of assistance to
you.

Yours sincerely,

B.Griffin,
Clinical Psychologist.

Bord Sláinte an Oirthir
Pt h Ospidéal Meabhairgalar
Dun Droma
Átha Cliath 14

Eastern Health Board
Central Mental Hospital
Dundrum
Dublin 14

Tel 98 43 28
Your ref
Our ref

1ˢᵗ June 1973

Secretary,
Department of Justice,
72/76 St. Stephen's Green,
Dublin 2.

Re: _____ James X _____

This is to state that we have this day examined
The above-named. In our opinions he is not now insane.

Dr. Peter Stevens
Physician and Governor

Dr. Tom Keegan
Senior Psychiatrist

Bord Sláinte an Oirthir
Ph...ch Ospidéal Meabhairgalar,
Dun Droma
Átha Cliath 14

Eastern Health Board
Central Mental Hospital
Dundrum
Dublin 14

Tel 98 43 28
Your ref
Our ref

1st June 1973

Dr Gilmartin,
Medical Officer,
St. Patricks Institution,
North Circular Road,

<u>Re:James X. aged 16 Private & confidential - not to be read in open court</u>

Dear Dr Gilmartin,

The above patient was first seen by me on 17th May, 1973 subsequent to which he was transferred to here by my suggestion. In the initial interview I was concerned by a number of features shown by the patient:-

(1)   A history of head injury in early childhood.

(2)   Treatment in a Child Guidance Clinic until recent months.

(3)   Bizarre features in the interview including delusional ideas of influence "possession and control by little men".

(4)   Convulsive tics during the interview accompanied by pallor and trembling

(5)   Homocidal fantasies with elaboration and suggestions of early implementation.

Since his hospitalization here he has been assessed by a consultant neurologist, who has not found any positive evidence of G.N.S. damage. Mr Griffin, Clinical Psychologist, has tested him and has found his verbal I.Q to be 98, his performance I.Q. to be 92 and his overall I.Q. to be 94 placing him in the average range of intellectual ability. Clinically however we all feel that James is a bright boy whose competence is not available to testing because of his relative lack of education. In the M.M.P.I. the most striking features evident were the high anxiety and antisocial score. He appears to have responded well to the hospitalization and now shows no evidence of psychosis or neurosis. His medication has included largactil but he is not on any at present.

<u>Impressions and Recommendations:</u>

James appears to belong to a delinquent sub-culture but appears capable of forming positive relationships. He is capable of clever and manipulative behaviour although there is evidence of severe neurosis it does not seem to me that he is psychotic. I believe that James is a disturbed boy and will merit future psychiatric help. Please do not hesitate to contact me about him in the future..

Yours sincerely,

P. Steens.

Dr Stevens M.B, M.A., M. O.Psych.,

79

GOVERNOR'S REPORT ON PUNISHMENT OF PRISONER

File B18/

2317/72.
ST PATRICKS INSTITUTION

Report on punishment imposed on Prisoner No. 4179/73
Name: James X, 2 Connolly House, Dublin
Officer responsible for report: Officer Mark Lawlor
Date of offence: 11.11.74

Nature of offence: Assaulting inmate 245 Des Ryan. Having entered his cell while he was absent and waited for him to return. (inmate 197 Les O'Brien was also in the cell getting toothpaste during this incident)

Prisoner's defence: "That's right. He was slagging my sister last night. I said nothing. He was there when I went in and was at toothpaste I think. I said 'say what you said last night' and he said 'fuck off'. I hit him a punch and he roared and Mr Lawlor come in. He told me to go to my cell. He's very aggravating and I went to the cell to give him a hiding".

Inmate Ryan. "we were slagging last night. He slagged my sister and I slagged his. I came back from washing, he was in my cell behind the door. He came out when I was hanging up my towel and caught me by the head and gave me a dig. There was another blow and Mr Lawlor came in. O'Brien had come in for a pin up that I'd promised him and was also in the cell when I came back. He had nothing to do with the fighting. Mr Lawlor pulled me out till X got out of my cell. I got two stitches over the right eye.

Inmate O'Brien. "We went in before Ryan came back. I was getting toothpaste from him and was in the cell first. X came after Ryan and struck Ryan. He said nothing. I just stood there. It only lasted a couple of seconds till Mr Lawlor came in and broke it up.

Punishment imposed by Governor: Forfeit remission & evening recreation for 14 days, the remission to take effect only in the event of any serious breach.

An Runaí
Roinn Dlí agus Cirt. Submitted, please. Form P.10 attached at Dept.

Martin O'Reilly

Governor   Date 13.11.'74

80

Freagraí chuig
   Oifigeach Promhaidh
Replies to
   Probation Officer
Teileafón 776831 Ext 10

AN tSEIRBHIS PHROMHAIDH
(The Probation Service)
5 CAISLEAN ÁTHA CLIATH
(5 Dublin Castle)
ÁTH CLIATH 2
(Dublin 2)

Institution No: 4179/73   9/11/'75

Dept No: B13/5561/72

Name: James X

Address: 2 Connolly House, Dublin.

Offence: Malicious Damage (pleaded not guilty)

Sentence: 3 years

Committal: 10.12.1973   Release: 3.4.76

This offender has had very little contact with our Service during sentence.
However he did come to our notice prior to this committal since he has a
substantial list of previous convictions, at least one of which is for
malicious damage.

I have spoken to him recently and have visited his home where conditions appear
to be much the same as those outlined in my report of 9.5.1973.

From my discussions with James, I am unable to alter my opinion that he has
not, to any great extent, changed his attitudes. He presents as a very
charming, plausible individual and is very much the exhibitionists when given
the opportunity.

This is his third Christmas in custody and in view of this and the facts that
he has completed most of his sentence and his relatively good behaviour here,
perhaps a short period of release at Christmas might be considered.

Enquiries from a Detective Inspector at Pearse Street Garda Station indicate
that James in considered to be a dangerous person, unless he has undergone a
substantial change for the better during this sentence.

The offender was recently permitted a period of temporary release to play in a
football game and responded satisfactorily to that.

In relation to Christmas Release I am of the opinion that, having regard to all
the information available to us, I could not go beyond recommending release for
some hours on Christmas day only. In his case, I consider that he should be
conveyed to and from his home by an official in order that for our part we
would minimalise the opportunity for him to ramble about the city.

His family would be very glad to have him home for Christmas.

D. Mangan (Welfare Officer).

81

Eis... agra uv an litir seo, is mar
seo ... choir e siuradh:—

Any reply to this communication
should be addressed to:—

An Rúnaí
(The Secretary)

ROINN DLÍ AGUS CIRT,
(Department of Justice),

72-76 FAICHE STIABHNA,
(72-76 St. Stephen's Green),

BAILE ÁTHA CLIATH, 2.
(Dublin, 2)

PSYCHOLOGICAL REPORT.

James X - aged 19   DATE OF TEST: 13/ 12 /'75

At the November meeting of the Liaison Committee, in St. Patrick's,
the case of James was discussed. It was suggested that James undergo
an aptitude test with a view to finding an occupational area into
which he might go after release.

James presented as a very pleasant and interesting young man. I saw
him on a few occasions. During the first test session he was
anxious to impress and spoke about his interest in reading and in
music. He seemed very interested in social problems, and had a good
understanding of his own background and the influence of the
environment on his deviant behaviour.

The aptitude test administered was the Differential Aptitude Test
Battery. It measures aptitudes in the following areas: verbal
reasoning, numerical ability, abstract reasoning, space relations,
and language usage. James's profile on this test shows a clear cut
lack of aptitude for all school, mechanical and engineering jobs.
There is only one aptitude where he shows a reasonable amount of
ability and that is Clerical Aptitude. But even here he is below
the average level for his age.

Consequently, the only area of work, as indicated by this test, that
is suitable for James is some fairly routine job that demanded some
clerical competence. Work of this kind would be typified by routine
filling of shelves in wholesale stores, checking labels, matching
prices etc. Since there is no evidence of mechanical reasoning
ability, the area of mechanics is not appropriate.

Unfortunately the Differential Aptitude Test battery does not
measure aptitudes in the artistic area, so there is no indication of
how well he might perform in the area of music.

Whatever, area of work or training James decided upon, it must be
remembered that his verbal reasoning, his numerical ability and his
abstract reasoning are very poor, and it is these aptitudes that
correlate with serious study in any area. So I recommend that James
be guided to a relatively unskilled type of work of the clerical
variety.

Psychologist,
Treatment of Offenders Division,
Dept. of Justice.

An Garda Síochána

Oifig Ginearálta
Slándáil agus Faisnéis
Ceanncheathrú na nGardaí
Páirc an Fhionn-Uisce
Baile Átha Cliath 8

General Office,
Security & Intelligence,
Garda Headquarters
Phoenix Park,
Dublin 8.

Records of James X – 2 Connolly House, Dublin.

Date: Metropolitan District Court 4 - 14/07/1976
Charge: **Simple Drunkeness**. Penalty: £2 fine

Date: Metropolitan District Court 4 -24/04/1977
Charge: **Drunk Breach of the Peace**. Penalty: £20 fine

Date: Metropolitan District Court 4 - 07/08/1978
Charge: **Loiter with intent**. Penalty: 3 Mths imprisonment – Mountjoy.

Date: Metropolitan District Court 4 – 25/04/1979
Charge: **Unlawful assault** (bailed 26/04/1979). Penalty: 3 Mths imprisonment – Mountjoy.

Date: Dublin District Court 6 - 16/02/1982
Charge: **Simple drunkenness** sec 15 Probation Act a 1842. Penalty: Fine £2

Date: DMA District Court Dun Laoghaire – 27/05/1983
Charge: **Simple Drunkeness**. Penalty: £1 Fine

Date: Dublin District Court 6 - 02/07/1983
Charge: **Drunk**. Penalty: £2 Fine

Date: Dublin District Court 6 - 19/04/1984
Charge: **Drunk**. Penalty: £3 Fine

Date: Metropolitan District Court 4 - 22/02/1985
Charge: **Malicious damage** Penalty: 6 Mths - Mountjoy – sentence suspended.

Date: Dublin District Court 6 - 13/07/1989 .
Charge: **Drunkness / breach of the peace**. Penalty: Bound to the Peace – 12Mths

Date: Dublin District Court 6 - 13/08/1990
Charge: **Breach of peace**. Penalty: £20 Fine, I Mth imprisonment – sentence suspended.

Date: Dublin District Court 6 - 15/10/1990
Charge: **Liquor licence act** Penalty: 7 days imprisonment – sentence suspended

Date: Dublin District Court 6 - 10/12/1991
Charge: **Breach of the peace / common assault**. Penalty: 1 Wk community care (60 hrs cso)

EAST COAST AREA HEALTH BOARD

Bord Sláinte Limistéar an Chósta Thoir

Mr James X
2 Connolly House,
Dublin.

24th June 2001

Dear Mr X,

I gave you all the information at my disposal. You must remember that record keeping was not a priority, generally in psychiatry when you were a patient. While the certification of insanity seems formal and stigmatising I can assure you that it was simply a transfer process by which persons in custody were moved into Dundrum. That was the way it was used then and viewed then and it's still that way retrospectively. What I am saying basically is that although you were certified as insane, insanity or madness was not necessarily validated by that opinion. Doctors use the certification process simply as a transfer document, that's the way it was. It is no longer so, but that will not relieve you I am sure. Equally the decertification process which again referred to insanity was no more than a transfer process back into the prison system. Obviously there is nothing in your clinical file to suggest insanity or psychosis. That's all I can reassure you of.

Yours sincerely,

Dr Peter Greene
Central Mental Hospital.

HIGH COURT SUMMONS

Between:

JAMES X

Plaintiff

-and-

THE STATE AND ITS SERVANTS AND AGENTS, THE CHURCH AND ITS SERVANTS AND AGENTS

Defendants

The Plaintiff's claim is for damages for personal injuries, mental distress, nervous shock, anguish, physical illness, loss, damage, inconvenience and expenses suffered and sustained by him by reason of the wilful assault and batter, physical abuse and trespass to the person of the plaintiff and negligence and breach of duty (including Statutory Duty) breach of Fiduciary Duty, breach of the Plaintiff's constitutional rights to Bodily Integrity, breach of Plaintiff's Constitutional Right to Education, breach of dominant position, breach of trust, and breach of the Defendants' obligations and duties as being in loco parentis of the Plaintiff, on the part of the Defendants and each or any of them, their servants and agents.

The Plaintiff's claim is brought herein pursuant to the Jurisdiction of Courts and Enforcement of Judgements Act, 1998 and the Convention Schedule thereto and under and by virtue of Article 5(3) section 2 title 2 thereof, this Honourable Court has jurisdiction in this matter.

Jurisdiction is conferred in this Honourable Court by the Article as the proceedings have their object matters relating to Court and the place where the harmful event occurred and which is a subject matter of the within proceedings was within the jurisdiction of this Honourable Court.

85